Where to Put Your Money

Where to Put Your Money

From £50 to £50,000

Jonathan Reuvid

**KOGAN
PAGE**

Introduction

Perhaps you've just had a windfall of a few hundred pounds or more from your premium bonds or a minor win on the National Lottery. Maybe a new job or salary rise has given you an extra £100 a month. In either case, unless you have set your mind on how to spend it immediately and, before you fritter it away on family expenditure, you may feel that you should consider where else to put your money.

Of course, you should. This book is written for those who've acquired a bit of spare cash, or even a sizeable lump, and want to use it sensibly. And, before you shy away from that forbidding word 'sensibly' – which you probably associate with school uniforms and skimmed milk – by closing the book and banishing it from sight, let's dispel some of the fog surrounding those buzzwords 'save' and 'spend'.

Save versus spend

Most of us have been brought up to believe that saving is 'good' and that spending, except on the bare necessities of life, is vaguely 'sinful'. This book explains why these perceptions are often false and why the distinction between 'save' and 'spend' is far from clear. Just two examples will show you what I mean.

Example 0.1

Putting your spare cash on deposit with your local friendly bank (some are more friendly than others) is generally regarded as prudent saving. But, when the rate of interest that the bank pays is less than the rate of inflation, as was the case some years ago in the United Kingdom, that form of saving is hardly prudent. Over the years, assuming that you leave the interest paid in the account, the amount of the accumulated deposit could well be less than the value of the original sum after inflation. (You will find out how to make the calculation yourself in Chapter 5.) In fact, you have suffered a loss in 'real' money terms. You thought that you were saving for a rainy day, but it started to drizzle from the moment you made your deposit.

Example 0.2

If you spend your spare cash now by purchasing in the summer sales at a deep discount household goods or clothes for the family that you know you will have to buy anyway in a few months' time, you really are saving money. That is what a prudent shopper does with 'special offers' every week. (In Chapter 1, we show you how to calculate simply whether you really are saving, after allowing for the cost of an extra trip to the discount store, which you might not make otherwise.)

What is saving really?

The trouble is, there is more than one definition. The *Oxford English Dictionary* gives two meanings for the noun 'saving': 1. Saving is 'an economy or reduction in money, time etc'. 2. Savings are 'money saved'.

None of us have any difficulty with the first definition. We know that in terms of our own money, saving generally means cutting cost by spending less. In this context, 'special offers' on essential items can be a big help when we 'spend to save'. This kind of saving through clever shopping is discussed in Part 1.

Another important way of saving your money is to repay expensive debt such as credit cards and personal loans with high interest costs and penalty charges. The real costs of expensive unsecured debt are revealed in Part 2.

The second definition, as we have seen in Example 0.1, is incomplete. Of course, if the only way that you can control your expenditure is by sticking it in the bank or elsewhere out of temptation's way – and most of us have that problem – then the dictionary has it right. In real terms, however, the value of your money is trickling away like an uncharged battery. Perhaps dictionary authors live on an inflation-free academic planet different from the real world that we inhabit.

This book is about extracting good value from your spare cash, and for that we offer another definition of saving: 'Saving is the deployment of money to generate increased value'. I've used the economist's rather fancy word 'deployment' to cover both low risk saving through cash account deposits and saving plans, including pensions and insurance, in Part 3; and more conventional financial investments in Part 4.

Some kinds of investment are really only suitable for rather larger sums of money. But, who knows? You may be about to receive a lump sum from your pension scheme on retirement or, less pleasantly, a substantial redundancy payment. Perhaps the finger of fate is about to point a major National Lottery prize in your direction.

In Part 5 we take a quick look at other kinds of investment that demand more active decisions by yourself, ranging from 'buy-to-let' property investment to forestry, from coloured diamonds to antiques and collectibles and even wine or horse racing bloodstock.

The last part of the book is a commentary on the realities of gambling in case you are tempted in that direction, and an overview of the scams and swindles to which savers and internet users are exposed.

Before you read on

One word of caution but encouragement to plunge into the detail of the chapters that follow. Beware of friendly advice. There will be plenty of advice around from friends and relations about where to put your money. Even if your best friend is an accountant or your uncle a bank manager – especially your uncle – remember that the money is yours and you are the only person who should decide. Remember, too, that it is a normal human reaction for people to tell you how clever they are with their investments (even when their share portfolio has had more failures than successes). By all means listen, but look before you leap.

There are two ways in which you can extract useful information from this book. You can glance at the table on the next page, which suggests which chapters to read depending on the amount of money you have available. Alternatively, I have included a 10-point checklist at the end of each chapter in Parts 1 to 5, giving a summary of the main points. If you think you know enough about a particular chapter topic, turn to the checklist at the end to see if there is anything you can add to your knowledge. If not, move on to the next chapter. Of course, you may miss out on some pearls of wisdom, but you can always come back for a second helping.

You owe it to yourself to understand how your money can be made to work for you. I hope you enjoy your fact-finding read.

Where to put your money – summary of suggestions

If you have…	Alternatives	Chapter
£50	An evening out. Buy something in the 'sales'.	1
	Visit your local betting shop.	14
£100	Avoid a late payment on a store card or credit card.	2, 3
	Buy premium bonds.	6
£1,000	Pay off a store card or deferred credit deal during the interest-free period.	2
	Pay into your most expensive credit card account.	3
	Invest in a tax-free ISA cash deposit for yourself or your child.	5
	If your children qualify, put more into their Child Trust Funds.	6
	Start buying collectibles at antique or flea markets.	12
£10,000	Pay off expensive debt.	2, 3, 4
	Invest up to the maximum £7,000 in your current year ISA.	5
	Put what's left into an instant access deposit account.	5
	Start a self-invested pension scheme (SIPP) if you don't have an occupational scheme.	7
£50,000	Pay off remaining expensive debt.	2, 3, 4
	Top up your SIPP and life assurance.	7
	Maximize your tax-free investments (ISAs, etc).	5
	Invest in low-risk bonds and fixed interest securities.	8
£100,000	Pay off all your non-mortgage debt.	2, 3, 4
	Invest most of your capital in low-risk fixed and index-linked bonds.	8
	Invest up to 10 per cent of your capital in unit trusts or open-ended investment companies (OEICs).	9
	Look at opportunities in UK 'buy-to-let' residential property.	11

Part One
Why cash is king

1 **Spending money wisely**

Extra spending isn't necessarily extravagant and, as noted in the Introduction, expenditure that saves money can make sense. So, put all feelings of guilt behind you and concentrate with me in this chapter on how to spend your windfall or extra income wisely.

Discount purchases

First, a few words on percentages and how not to be fooled by them. We are all prone to self-deception and some retailers of goods and services do a good job in confusing us into believing that we are making a bigger cash saving than is the case.

Example 1.1

An identical electric iron (same brand and same model) is offered at a discount in two stores, 'A' and 'B', at the following prices:

	Usual retail price	Discount
Store A	£22.00	10% off
Store B	£20.00	5% off

At first sight Store A offer sounds the more generous. But work it out in cash terms and see what the offers really mean:

	Store A	Store B
Usual retail price	£22.00	£20.00
Less discount	2.20	1.00
Actual net price	£19.80	£19.00

And so, the lesson from that simple exercise is 'Don't trust percentages' or to put it in more familiar terms – adapted to today's shopping world – 'If you look after the pounds and pence, the percentages will take care of themselves'.

Of course, there are more subtle examples of deceptive pricing; manufacturers of washing machine powders and dishwasher tablets can be particularly sneaky. They commonly introduce differences in weight when framing their 'special offers', which make it harder to calculate the true unit price.

Example 1.2
A famous brand of washing powder 'FADE' normally offers its products in alternative packet sizes of 115 grams and 460 grams, priced as follows:

	115g packet	460g packet
Normal store price	£2.10	£6.00

It's easy to calculate that four small packets cost £8.40 against £6.00 for one large packet containing the same amount. And so there is a £2.40 (or 28.5 per cent) real saving in purchasing a large packet. However, things become more complicated with this FADE special offer:

'BUY TWO SMALL PACKS FOR THE PRICE OF ONE OR ONE-THIRD OFF NORMAL PRICE'

There are now three alternatives at reduced prices:

	115g	2 × 115g	460g
Offer price	£1.40	£2.10	£4.00

It's easy to see that buying two packs for one is equivalent to a single pack price of £1.05, but ' two for one' means '50 per cent off' and that sounds better than 'one-third off' for the larger pack. However, four packets (460g) on the two for one basis now costs £4.20, which is still more expensive than the discounted 460g packet.

Of course, that was not a real example and often special offers are more complicated. Sometimes, there are three packet sizes and the weights are not exact multiples of each other. If the large pack size had been 450g, you would have had to be a mathematician to work out the exact difference in your head. Some supermarkets, but by no means all, show a unit price in small print on the shelf ticket but even that may be only occasional.

This sort of special offer is legal because it doesn't offend any of the trading laws and is not classified legally as misleading, although you and I might think otherwise. However, it does explain why on Saturday mornings at my local supermarket, there are shoppers crouched in clusters in front of the bottom shelves of the washing powder section with their calculators.

Most discounting is much more straightforward than these examples suggest where the retailer shows the 'old price' (often with a line through it) and the new price below it. No more than common sense is required here but there are differences in the decision process that you can apply depending on the type of goods.

Consumables

Consumables – basically food, drink, household cleaning products, toiletries, baby products, petfoods and some clothes – are the products that find their way regularly into the family shopping basket. The rational decision process is quite complicated:

▌ Would I buy it anyway?
 – In the case of food, would we consume it before the 'eat by' date, or can it be frozen?
 – Is there room in our fridge/freezer?
 – How often would I buy it normally?
 – At the cheaper price, would we use/eat it more often?
 – Is it likely to be discounted again soon?
▌ Is it a substitute for a product that we use normally?
 – Shall I buy it because it is cheaper than the product we normally buy (the most frequent factor in switching to supermarket own brands)?
 – Shall I buy it because it is a preferred product that is normally too expensive (a good reason for a treat)?
 – Shall I buy it because it's something we don't have normally, and I know we would enjoy trying it (fine, but don't pretend that you are saving)?

Whoever said that shopping was simple?

Consumer durables

These range from clothing, bedclothes, soft furnishings, audio, video and digital tapes, CDs, garden tools and sports equipment to *capital goods* – more substantial items of expenditure for the home, such as white goods (refrigerators, freezers, washing machines, cookers, etc); other electrical and electronic products (from kettles and vacuum cleaners to TV sets, mobile telephones and PCs); furniture, kitchen and bathroom fittings; major items of garden equipment; bicycles, motorcycles and even motor cars.

There's an important distinction between consumer durables, which are often purchased for cash, and capital goods, where buying on credit is more common. Of course, if you've just gained a major cash windfall you are more likely to purchase your new motor car for cash, but for most of us some kind of credit agreement or loan is inevitable. The management of credit cards, loans and other methods of funding capital goods acquisitions are discussed in Chapter 3.

We are more likely to buy consumer durables, rather than capital goods, at so-called 'factory outlets' or the increasingly frequent seasonal sales: January sales, spring sales, summer sales, winter sales and, last December as a reflection of poor high street trading conditions, pre-Christmas sales. The decision factors for factory outlet shopping and 'the sales' are discussed in the next section.

For now, in relation to discount bargains on consumable and low value consumer durables, there's just one more factor that shoppers tend to overlook or, perhaps, choose to ignore – the travel cost of making special trips to take advantage of low price offers. Whether you travel by bus, train, taxi or motor car that extra trip to the supermarket or discount store has a cost. Even if you bicycle or walk, there is a notional but negligible cost of tyre rubber or shoe leather.

Maybe you'll say that I'm splitting hairs but think of it this way. Suppose that you decided to take advantage of that special offer in Example 1.1, to make an extra trip to buy that electric iron from Store B at a saving of £1.00. Store B is three miles away so that you make a six-mile round trip by car. The Automobile Association will tell you that the cost of using the normal family saloon is at least 35p a mile to include depreciation, insurance and maintenance as well as the cost of petrol, so that you are about to spend £2.10 to make a saving of £1.00. Unless you will be using a company car, leave it in the garage and wait until you pass by on a normal shopping trip. It may even be worth buying from store A, if that is where you make your usual weekly shop.

Factory outlets

Out of town shopping centres, in which the 'factory outlets' of famous brands (particularly those of international fashion clothing designers that have their own city centre shops) open or license boutiques where they offer their own products cut-price, have become a popular feature of the UK shopping scene. Other types of branded premium products, such as watches, silver and jewellery, glass, china and tableware have adopted the same new channels to market. The pressures on the retail outlets to sell high volumes are high; typically, the terms of occupation are a rental charge for the space occupied and a percentage of turnover paid to the site owner and operator plus the cost of fitting out and decorating the shop. The leases are short and retailers, however famous the brand name, that fail to generate target revenue for the site owner, are dumped. Some well-known retailers, as well as manufacturers, also have outlets at which more than one brand is stocked but the same tough rules on revenue performance apply.

Bicester Village, off the M40, in Oxfordshire is a successful example of factory outlet trading. The psychological pressure on visiting shoppers to buy is also quite intense. To begin with, most shoppers have made a special outing to visit the 'Village', which involves an allocation of time as well as travel cost. (On my calculation the round trip from London and back involves 120 miles motoring or a minimum of £42 cost – much more for Porsches or petrol-thirsty off-roaders.) So, there is an incentive to hunt down at least one major bargain rather than leave empty-handed. Then, the shopping environment is attractive: quite small, separate units in a clean, broad 'village street' layout with coffee shops and quality fast food outlets. And the sight of fellow shoppers strolling along with brightly coloured shiny shopping bags bearing brand logos is usually a turn on for most of us.

The problems come with the merchandise itself and the pricing. First, the products. Here are some questions to ask yourself, if you are shopping for clothes:

▌ The branding may be that of your favourite Italian fashion house that normally you can only gawp at in the pages of the glossies, but is the garment from this year's range or simply something that they couldn't sell last year? (On the other hand, does it matter if the price is really low?)

▌ Is the garment part of the manufacturer's regular line anyway? Some fashion houses run two labels under the same brand: perhaps one colour label for the superior quality line and one for a lower 'standard' quality line. If you are buying the top label at a discount, there should be no quality concerns. But some manufacturers commission special lower quality lines for their factory outlets, which never appear in their regular ranges and for which they think there is a current popular demand. They carry the brand, possibly the secondary label, and are sold at very cheap prices. Often the quality is inferior; so bargain hunters beware.

▌ Another frequent occurrence in factory outlets and all kinds of manufacturers' sales is the offer of 'seconds', which are claimed to be the normal stock in a flawed condition (some small mark, stitching error or snag in the weave), which justifies the price reduction. That may be so, but instead could it be part of a poor batch of garments from an inferior, secondary supplier? Seconds are more common in men's clothes, particularly shirts and shoes, but be sure to compare with the standard article of clothing. Only inspection will tell whether the general manufacturing quality and material are genuine.

Then there is the issue of price. Typically, the products on display will carry price labels showing two or even three prices: the original or recommended retail price (RRP), which should be the price on the same garment when it was offered for sale in the manufacturer's normal city centre or high street outlet (for example, Bond Street or Sloane Street if sold in London), the factory outlet price and perhaps a third 'sale price'. The earlier prices are usually crossed through – but still readable. Sometimes, there will be a notice above a rack of clothes saying 'X per cent off last price'. All these prices should be inclusive of VAT (although that is not always the case with capital goods).

Such pricing is completely fair and above board, but you need to focus on the final price and decide whether you can afford it and whether it is good value for money to you personally. For example, a designer dress that originally retailed at £2,700, was offered first for £1,800 (one-third off) at the factory outlet, then slashed to £1,200 (55 per cent off original price) and finally discounted in the sale to £800 (one-third off last price) represents a terrific reduction of £1,900. But don't kid yourself that you are saving £1,900 if you buy it. If the maximum you normally pay for a dress is £80 or perhaps a bit more, you are being extravagant. Without question.

On the other hand, it's your windfall and your money. If you want the dress for a special occasion and you're sure that it won't go out of fashion or that you will wear it again and again (or at least convince yourself that is true), go ahead and splurge. Don't let me put you off by telling you that when you go back next week the other dress – the one you liked almost as much – may be down to £500.

'The sales'

The same considerations of product quality and price apply to bargain hunting in the high street seasonal sales. However, department stores and multiples in cities and the larger towns have a bewildering variety of products on offer at rock bottom prices across a wide range of consumer durables, including capital goods, as well as consumables. The practice of buying in large quantities of special 'sale goods' with customer appeal, often own branded but of rather low quality and usually for the younger adult sectors, is widespread among the bigger stores and retail groups.

However, one factor that distinguishes department store sales from other retail outlets is the need to sell off stocks of poor selling lines, particularly higher value lines of capital goods such as white goods and furniture, so that it is possible to buy genuinely worthwhile items, sometimes on credit or 'easy payment' terms.

Irresistible bargains

Because the price cuts in high street seasonal sales are even deeper than at factory outlets (and for less exotic clothing items too), it is easy to make a quite different kind of bad buying decision. Clothes priced originally at £50 and above can often be purchased for £10 or less, which won't strain even a modest budget.

There's just one problem. Are you sure that you are buying the garment because you like it and really want it, or just because it's cheap?

The irresistible bargain that you buy for a ridiculously cheap price may seem just ridiculous when you get it home. Whatever possessed you to buy a colour or a neckline that you know doesn't suit you? And when would you ever wear it? If it is destined to hang at the back of your wardrobe without ever being worn, then the purchase was a mistake. Not just an extravagance, but a waste. Fortunately, there is always your local charity shop and they are unlikely to turn down anything as a gift.

Purchasing online or by mail order

Until the internet revolution, time was that home shopping was conducted almost exclusively by ordering by mail or telephone from catalogues or by direct response to advertisements and loose inserts in the national Press and consumer magazines. Customers could pay either by sending a cheque or quoting their credit card number on the written order sent in the post or given over the telephone.

Now the new technology has broadened the methods by which we can order and pay remotely for goods; in some cases direct from the manufacturer, in others from the direct mail retailer. Written, signed orders can be placed by fax with credit card details. Alternatively, orders can be placed by e-mail via the internet or on the retailer's own internet website.

From the manufacturer's or retailer's point of view, use of the internet has opened up effective new channels to market. Retailers can continue to advertise special offer sales deals in the Press or by direct mail to existing and identified potential customers, but they can also advertise them on the internet, placing the full details including product pictures or photographs on their websites, or e-mailing direct to established customers inviting them to visit their websites.

One enormous advantage for the seller, whatever kind of direct order is placed, is that he or she receives payment before accepting and fulfilling the order. Since delivery times from receipt of order of up to three weeks are accepted by customers as commonplace for some goods, retailers who are not manufacturers don't necessarily have to hold stock themselves and, once a significant and regular flow of orders has built up, may even be able to trade with their marketing costs covered by a positive cash flow.

The advantages for you, the consumer, are less clear-cut and you should ask yourself the following questions:

■ How do the prices online or by direct mail compare with those at retail outlets (don't forget to add in post and packaging – P&P – if charged)?

■ How does the quality of the products compare (you probably won't know until you take delivery)?

■ If I don't like what I get, can I send it back without penalty (you won't get the P&P back unless the goods were defective)?

■ Do I get the full benefit of manufacturers' guarantees available when sold through a shop (more important for consumer durables other than clothes where inspection usually tells all)?

Subject to these questions, clothes purchased online or by mail order are usually good value. Now that this channel to market has become extremely competitive, delivery times are greatly reduced – down to three days from some suppliers. You may find that sizes are not quite what you expected, but that doesn't matter too much if you can return the goods readily.

Purchasing some consumer durables in this way, particularly personal computers, can be less satisfactory. One global market leader in PCs that advertises widely by direct mail and flyer inserts in newspapers, as well as on the internet, offers especially tempting bargains on its own brand of high specification products together with deferred payment terms, subject to credit standing. However, a telephone call to the manufacturer's call centre, located somewhere in Asia, reveals that all is not what it seems. There are additional items of software at extra cost, which you are told are essential to connect to your server or Broadband, and only 'interest-free' credit rather than deferred payment (see Chapter 2) is available to your category of customer. Nothing quite illegal, but as the lawyers say, 'caveat emptor', which translates simply from the Latin to 'let the buyer beware'. In the face of this kind of doubtful practice you may well wonder whether you want to do business. If you're like me, you take the decision to junk unread all further mail shots and flyers that you may receive from that supplier.

You do have special rights in law now if you are purchasing online or, indeed, by mail order. If you want to be sure what these rights are you should consult *Consumer Protection (Distance Selling) Regulations 2000* published by The Stationery Office Books (ISBN: 0 1109 9872 3) in paperback at £3.50.

Paying by cash

We are told that paying cash is the most satisfactory way of buying something we want. By 'cash' we mean payment in currency (notes and coins), by cheque or by bank debit card where the equivalent pounds and pence are transferred from your account to that of the seller. Of course, if you are using a bank overdraft for the payment by cheque or debit card, that is not quite the same thing and you will incur interest at whatever rate your bank charges you for the use of your overdraft. We will discuss bank overdrafts and loans in Chapter 4.

If you don't have the money now in your bank account, one alternative is to save up until you do and the different ways in which you can save cash instalments over a period of time are reviewed in Part 3. Bank deposit accounts and savings accounts also provide interest that is credited to your account with continuing interest on the accumulated balance.

Checklist

1. Don't be fooled by percentages in discount offers. It's the pounds and pence of the net selling price that count.
2. When it comes to bargain prices on consumables (the weekly shopping basket), ask yourself two sets of questions: would I buy it anyway, and is it a substitute for a product you use normally?
3. With consumer durables, distinguish between cash and credit purchases. Consult Chapter 2 to discover the landmines in buying on credit.
4. Take into account the travel cost of extra shopping trips to buy bargains.
5. Be careful at factory outlets and seasonal sales with fashion clothes that are out of date (or are about to be). Check that the garments on offer are from the manufacturer's regular lines and not just bought in for discount outlets. Take care with 'seconds' too.
6. If you decide to spend your windfall on a high quality fashion garment at a rock bottom price, but still well above the price you would consider paying normally, be sure that you will get wear out of it. Then go ahead and splurge.

7. Beware of the irresistible bargain that you hate once you inspect it in the cold light of day and consign to the back of your cupboard. That's not extravagance, but waste.
8. Online and mail order purchasing is often fine, especially for clothes, if you can be sure of being able to return goods without penalty, prompt delivery and price comparability.
9. With consumer durables, particularly PCs, when buying online or by telephone watch out for sneaky practices: pressure selling of 'essential' extras not included in the offer or credit terms that are not what they seemed.
10. If you decide to save up before buying, make good use of savings or bank deposit accounts to earn interest that accumulates.

2 Buying on credit

Buying on credit usually adds greatly to the cost of purchase but there are several kinds of credit account that can be used without penalty, if you are careful. Others, as we shall see are much more dangerous. In this chapter we explore the various kinds of credit that are available to you at the point of sale other than credit cards, which are discussed thoroughly in Chapter 3.

Monthly accounts

Until the 1980s, when plastic began to make serious inroads into high street shopping and before the IT revolution, it was quite common for shops and stores to offer their regular customers monthly accounts. Monthly accounts were available in village stores or in larger shops in the towns and cities, even at rural petrol stations to local residents. They were not available in supermarkets. The advantage that they brought to customers, as well as deferred payment, was that they could carry less cash and avoid writing cheques. For retailers, the monthly account was an effective means of attracting customer loyalty and of combating price sensitivity. For village shops, in particular, the lure of low supermarket prices in the local shopping centre could be offset only by providing convenience and the monthly account was a part of that offering.

The basis of the monthly credit account is that the retailer makes up a statement on a given day each month, which is posted to the customer for payment during the month following. Typically, the statement is marked 'settlement within 30 days' or by a specified date. Some world-weary retailers who cater for customers who don't pay on time specify 'settlement within 15 days' in the hope that 30-day payment will be achieved.

This kind of account has largely disappeared. Retailers prefer to take plastic: store cards, in the case of major stores or retail chains, credit cards or, best of all, bank debit cards. The cost of processing the transaction is borne by the retailer but that is the price of assured and prompt payment. Even in the countryside, the new forms of electronic payment are almost universal. When we buy the weekend joint and a few dozen eggs at our local farmshop, it is fully equipped with the latest 'swipe' and PIN card equipment. Only my local newspaper agent who delivers daily has maintained monthly accounts for the households on his round but, as an ex-policeman he can feel reasonably certain that he will get paid.

The monthly accounts that do remain, mainly city and major town centre stores, operate with more discipline. Customers are now required to sign direct debit mandates (DDs) on their bank accounts so that the retailer can claim the full amount shown on the previous month's statement at a specified date in the month following. Your bank is obliged to pay the DD provided that there is sufficient credit on your current account. If the DD is rejected you still have to pay and are likely to lose your monthly account facility as well.

Effectively, if you purchase goods on your monthly account on the first day of the new month you will not have to pay for them for nearly two months, typically 56 days. Therefore, if you are offered a monthly credit account and you are confident of being able to pay off amounts due, you should probably open it.

Loyalty cards

Loyalty cards do not provide credit but are often a first step towards store cards that do. In order to avoid confusion, we review here what they are and how they work.

Supermarkets and some other retailers offer their customers a loyalty card, which they can present at the cash-out and, when swiped through the till, award bonus points according to the value of the transaction. The bonus points for that transaction and accumulated bonus points are shown on the bottom of the till receipt. The retailer can also offer additional bonus points on the purchase of individual items from time to time as a form of special offer instead of (or as well as) a discounted price that are added on to the transaction.

Two of the best-known loyalty cards are Tesco's Clubcard and Sainsbury's Reward Card, which is now merged into 'Nectar', a composite loyalty card used by an informal grouping of diverse retail outlets that have combined together to market special offers across a wide range of goods and services. Both Tesco and Sainsbury issue quarterly newsletters to their loyalty cardholders, accompanied by special offers and money-off coupons on selected products, which may be used on your regular shopping trips. However, Tesco and Sainsbury offer different ways for you to redeem your bonus points. Tesco will send you a cash voucher once a quarter with your newsletter, which you can redeem at the cash-out next time you shop there. Sainsbury is more flexible; you can cash in all or just some of the bonus points that you have accumulated from previous transactions at the cash-out as an offset to the total cost of your current shopping visit.

Loyalty cards are what they say. You gain a small discount on your total purchases from the store or others in the same chain and they encourage you to spend more there rather than elsewhere. But don't be misled by bonus points on selected items, which may persuade you to buy one brand rather than another, or more than you would normally. Be sure to factor in the value of the points against any price or quality advantage in the alternatives. Money-off coupons can mislead too; sometimes they are offered on a product above your usual price range, for example, bottles of wine. We are back into the spending wisely territory of Chapter 1. Be sure that it is something you really want or like. However, loyalty cards are largely harmless.

Store cards

We are now entering shark-infested waters. If loyalty cards are harmless, store cards can be harmful and may seriously damage your economic health. At its simplest, a store card is a credit card that you can only use in particular stores – the branded store that issues the card to you.

However enticing the discount offered on your shopping, you should understand that the interest rates that store card operators charge on balances beyond the interest-free period are often exorbitant and are generally higher than the rates charged by the better credit cards and much dearer by comparison with the cost of an overdraft or personal bank loan. Typically, store card interest is charged at 26 to 30 per cent annual percentage rates (APRs) equivalent to around six times the Bank of England base rate at 1 January 2005. More modest rates are offered by some chains including John Lewis and Waitrose and Marks & Spencer, but still higher than most general credit cards.

Like the old-fashioned monthly account, the store card allows you interest-free credit on purchases up to an average of 56 days, but you are immediately subject to the high interest rates on purchases when you stray beyond the free credit period. You will also suffer late payment charges (£15 by Marks & Spencer according to the December 2004 issue of *Which?* magazine) but these are often concealed in the small print of the accompanying agreement. *Which?* questioned how many of the United Kingdom's 14 million store cardholders were aware of the cost of using them. Following a pre-Christmas survey in London's Oxford Street, *Which?* found that even the people selling them don't always know the interest rate and other charges.

There's a further peril from store cards, of which you should be aware. Some store card companies send unsolicited cheques to cardholders to encourage them to borrow more on their cards. Avoid them like the plague and tear them up if you're tempted. If you cash such a cheque the interest rate applied will be raised to include a cash handling fee of, for example, 1.5 per cent of the value of the cheque in a case cited by *Which?*. In that particular case, the overall interest rate charged was a jaw-dropping 32.8 per cent. Look up the meaning of the word 'usury' in your dictionary and see if you think it applies.

The highly recommended action on store card debt that you can't pay off from your bank current account is to switch it to a cheaper general credit card or, better still, to a bank personal loan account.

If you want to take the trouble, you can outwit the store card company by opening the account, taking the discount offered on your first purchase, then paying off the debt within the interest-free period and shredding the card.

About interest rates

It may come as a shock to you but there are no effective limits yet on the interest rates that credit cards or store cards can charge. The review of the Consumer Credit Act in 2004 addressed some issues such as extortionate lending, but it has failed to deal with the differences in the methods of calculating interest. In Chapter 3 we'll look at some of the rapacious ways in which credit card companies calculate interest rates and allocate payments. For now, an explanation of what is meant by APR and how it applies to store cards and in-store credit may be helpful.

The APRs that companies quote are supposed to help you compare different credit deals. Sometimes flat rates are quoted by the same lender as well, which are lower than APRs. The reason for the difference is that the APR takes into account the dates when you pay interest and charges and how you pay them, as well as the repayment dates for the money that you have borrowed. Flat rates do not take these facts into account and can mislead you as to the true cost of borrowing. If both rates are quoted the APR should be shown more prominently. How interest charges are applied differs from one company to another and important information is only given in the small print of a credit agreement in language that may seem obscure, even unintelligible.

The Financial Services Authority, which is the government watchdog over all providers of financial services, empowered only a few years ago, also has teeth and can levy hefty fines on companies and their directors in all parts of the industry. So far it has focused heavily on the sellers of endowment assurance and pension schemes and has fined companies in that sector heavily. It is not unlikely that consumer credit suppliers will come under a more searching spotlight soon and that the FSA will start to penalize those that it considers to be exploiting the consumer unfairly or dishonestly.

In the meantime, we have no choice but to continue with what is on offer, but be sure to shop around and evaluate and compare the different types of credit that are on offer.

In-store credit

Retailers of carpets, furniture, electrical items, particularly high ticket items from cookers and all white goods to TV sets, other audio-visual equipment and PCs, often offer credit deals to help you 'buy now and pay later' for your purchases and enjoy their use immediately. Some of these deals are genuinely attractive, but others can be even more expensive than the store card credit that we have just discussed.

Deferred payment deals

Deferred payment allows you to set up a loan agreement when you purchase to defer payment until six or 12 months after the date of purchase. Provided that you pay off the whole of the balance at or before the end of the deferred payment period, you incur no interest. However, if you do not repay you will be charged interest back to the original date of purchase and for the full term of the loan. When you sign the agreement you will also sign a DD mandate, which enables the lender to claim monthly payments from your bank after the interest-free period for the duration of the loan. APRs are generally in the range of 29 to 30 per cent. An actual example of what happened and what could have happened highlights the benefits and the pitfalls of such arrangements:

Example 2.1 – 'Buy now pay later' personal loan agreement

In November 2003, Sandra decided to buy a new electric cooker from the local outlet of a well-known branded discount store. The store assistant offered her a credit agreement from a consumer finance bank with a deferred payment arrangement, which gave her the option to discharge the loan agreement at the original cash price of the cooker up to 12 months from the month of purchase. If she did not pay it off during the period, then she would pay off the debt plus interest over 37 months by direct debit. Sandra signed the DD mandate at the same time as the loan agreement.

The details of the transaction were shown in a schedule on the front page of the agreement:

Description of goods/services	Cash price inc. VAT (£)
Cooker	479.98
Install & scrap old cooker	59.95
Extended five-year warranty	115.00
Total cash price of goods/services	654.93
Less deposit payable to the supplier	0.00
Amount of credit	654.93
Number of monthly repayments	37
Total amount payable £1218.04	29.5% APR
(total charge for credit £563.11)	
Monthly repayment amount	32.95

Sandra was also offered payment protection insurance (PPI) covering Life, Sickness, Accident and Unemployment, which she did not take. Had she done so there would have been an addition of 13.79 per cent (£4.54) to the monthly repayment amount.

Shortly after taking delivery, Sandra received the first of two letters from the bank confirming the repayment option and the monthly DD arrangements. She received a second letter shortly before expiry of the repayment option explaining how and when the DD would be claimed. Sandra repaid the total cash price before the due date.

No harm was done in Sandra's case. However, had she overstepped the option period, interest at 29.5 per cent APR would have been charged back to the date of signature of the agreement and the total charge of £563.11 would have amounted to a monster 86 per cent of the total cash price. The backdating was spelt out only in the (very) small print on the second page of the personal loan agreement.

One more uncomfortable feature of this 'buyer beware' story is that Sandra found that she could only repay the debt by sending a cheque by post. The finance house would not accept a credit card or bank debit card payment. And that meant that Sandra had to ask her husband to write a cheque on his current account.

Interest-free deals

The waters become decidedly murkier when we look at the so-called 'interest-free' deals that some retailers offer as alternatives to deferred payment. Sometimes they are advertised as '0 per cent finance' and they are harder to escape from unharmed than the deal described above.

As before, you are invited to take advantage of an interest-free period of six to 12 months by signing a personal loan agreement with a consumer finance house and a DD mandate. However, this time you are required to make monthly payments during the interest-free period, which are normally set so that there is still a balance outstanding as the repayment option expires. Unscrupulous retailers set low monthly repayments, which you are not allowed to increase and won't accept intermediate lump sums to ensure that the balance remaining is still substantial.

Again, if you repay the balance in full during the option period you will escape free. If not, interest at 27 to 30 per cent APR is charged back to the date you signed the agreement. The Office of Fair Trading has pressed retailers to stop advertising these deals as 'interest-free' and some, such as Allied Carpets, Comet, Dixons Group, Furnitureland, Harveys Furnishings, Powerhouse and Time Computers have all complied. However, some still offer the same deals under a new name such as Powerhouse's 'interest opt-out flexible finance'. Weasel words you may think – but I couldn't possibly comment.

Before you sign a deal of this kind, you should find out what methods you can use to repay the loan later and whether there are any repayment penalties. If you are going to buy a high value item, you should explore other forms of credit such as a personal loan from your bank or one of the lower interest credit cards described in Chapter 3.

In-store personal loans

Generally, personal loans on offer from retailers are also expensive although not quite as exorbitant as their 'interest-free' deals. Currys, Dixons, Harveys Furnishings, PC World and Time Computers all charge more than 19 per cent APR. However, some stores, such as Furnitureland and Harveys Furnishings do offer genuine 0 per cent APR loans on some products from time to time.

Checklist

1. Old-fashioned monthly accounts give you up to 56 days free credit and are fine. In their modern form, be careful that your bank current account can stand the DD for last month's purchases.
2. Loyalty cards are harmless and do give you a small discount via their bonus points. But don't be misled by bonus points on particular items or money-off coupons that tempt you into buying a more expensive alternative to your normal choice.
3. Store cards are dangerous unless you pay off the balance outstanding within the interest-free period. When you stray over the free credit period you will be charged interest at up to 30 per cent APR. You may also be hit with late payment charges.
4. If you are a store cardholder, be sure to tear up any unsolicited cheque you receive as a cash advance against your account. If used, the handling fee could raise the interest rate charged to as much as 32.8 per cent.
5. Interest rates and their calculation are not effectively controlled by law. Always look at the APRs quoted, which include interest and other charges, as well as the timing of payments. They are comparable between credit suppliers. Flat rates are not.
6. 'Buy now pay later' deals may be attractive but compare the different types of credit on offer. The better credit cards, overdrafts and personal bank loans are definitely cheaper than store cards or in-store deals.

7. Deferred credit deals are useful to ease your cash flow provided that you pay the debt back in full during the option period. If not, you will be charged interest back to the start date at up to 30 per cent APR for the full period of the loan, collected monthly by DD.

8. 'Interest free' or '0 per cent finance' deals can be sneaky. Look out for low monthly repayment instalments in the six to 12 months when no interest is charged that leave you with a balance on the loan at the end of the initial period that you can't pay off. If you don't pay it off, interest will be charged at 27 to 30 per cent APR back to the date of signature and recovered by DD.

9. Personal loans offered by retailers are also expensive, typically more than 19 per cent. Go for a personal loan from your bank or one of the lower cost credit cards instead.

10. Before signing a credit deal of any kind check out if you can repay the loan at any time without penalty and, if not, what the early settlement charges might be.

Part Two

Borrowing – benefit or burden?

3 Credit cards

In Chapter 2 we reviewed some painless and some quite painful methods of taking credit from suppliers. Now, it's time to move on to the most frequently used form of plastic payment – the credit card. Credit cards have become a part of our daily life and have changed our spending habits irrevocably. Like all addictive habits, it becomes very difficult to break free of the circle of spending and debt in which credit cards encourage us to indulge.

The temptation to overspend, and therefore incur monthly payments that we can't really afford, is fuelled by regular offers to raise your credit limit, if you are a good payer, and by frequent invitations to take on new credit cards, as more and more consumer credit companies enter the market. This chapter attempts to guide you on selecting the best credit card deals, some of the tricks that this part of the credit industry uses to increase its profits at your expense and how to manage your credit cards.

Comparing credit cards

You might think that making a choice is simply a matter of comparing interest and charges on a like-for-like basis, but you would be wrong. Credit card companies calculate interest in different ways, which makes it almost impossible to compare the true cost of their cards.

The difficulty arises because the start and stop dates for charging interest vary from card to card. Two credit cards that *Which?* magazine identified in its January 2005 issue both had an APR interest rate of 15.9 per cent, but because of the differences in timing, the calculated interest charges of one were much greater (40 per cent more) than the other. Of course, APR interest rates vary widely from around 9 per cent up to 18 per cent among mainstream card companies and wildly up to 31 per cent for some fringe operators.

In another example, the APR interest charges of two further cards are quoted as 9.9 per cent and 13.9 per cent. *Which?* calculated that if you spend £300 on each card in one month and pay £100 when you get your bill; then spend £150 more in the following month and pay off the next bill in full when you receive it, the charges would be identical. As in the case of discount pricing, discussed in Chapter 1, sometimes nothing is quite what it seems.

There has been intense lobbying to standardize the way in which interest is calculated, but the industry reply is that standardization would discourage competition. A likely story! We have to hope that the FSA's continuing scrutiny of the credit industry will result in regulation to standardize interest calculation, but until then you cannot choose your credit card by simply comparing APR interest rates.

However, you can compare terms and conditions and the other charges that credit card companies impose, although this may be quite an 'eyes down' job. Your final choice of card may also be affected by your own payment habits, whether you are likely to benefit from 'cashback' and whether you want to use your card for foreign transactions when you are abroad on holiday or business. If you want to study the options in detail for a wide range of cards, an excellent source of information on the internet is www.which.co.uk/creditcards (subscribers only but free trial available).

Interest-free period

Before we move on to other types of charges, it's useful to understand the advantages and limitations of the 'interest-free period' that some companies trumpet loudly in their promotions.

As in the case of monthly accounts and store cards discussed in Chapter 2, if you make a purchase the day your statement arrives, billing will be made on the next month's statement and there will be a few weeks to pay. There could be as long as 59 days before interest is charged from the date of the transaction. The actual length of time before interest is charged depends on how long you have in which to pay from receipt of the statement. Some give only 14 days but the best offer 25 days. In some cases, credit card companies don't actually mail their statements until three days after the statement date, which gives you even less time to pay before interest is charged.

Zero interest offers

It has become common for card companies to offer you a '0 per cent' rate on purchases for an introductory period in order to tempt you to take up their cards. They may also offer you the opportunity to transfer a balance from another card and pay no interest on the amount transferred for a limited period, typically six months. For example, if you transfer a balance of £5,000 from a card charging interest at 14.9 per cent you can save £350 over six months.

But, before you jump on the first zero interest offer that drops through your letterbox, you should understand how card companies use the payments you make to pay off your debt. If the new card company gives you a 0 per cent deal on your transferred balance but charges interest, say at 14.9 per cent, on new purchases, it will probably use the payments it receives to pay off the lowest rate debt first, that is the balance transferred at 0 per cent, before paying off your new purchases.

Also, be careful that no 'commission' is charged (perhaps 2 per cent) on accepting your transferred balance at 0 per cent interest. Like some of the interest-free deals we looked at in Chapter 2, if there is a charge, it is not a genuine 0 per cent offer.

As at December 2004, HSBC, Nationwide, Liverpool Victoria and Saga all pay off your most expensive debt first, but they were the exception. The optimum is a deal that offers 0 per cent for a period on both purchases and balance transfers with a low rate of interest subsequently.

Card charges

Penalty charges are made when you pay your bill late or exceed your credit limit, typically at £20 or £25 each time. When last checked, several credit card companies, such as Bank of Ireland Moneyback MasterCard, Lombard Direct MasterCard, and Nationwide charge less. Liverpool Victoria Visa and Saga Visa charge £10 penalty fees and Bank of Ireland MasterCard makes no charge at all, although it charges a higher rate of interest at 18.9 per cent. Abbey does not charge its £25 penalty the first time you pay late. The best way to avoid late payment charges altogether is to set up a monthly direct debit for the minimum payment (or full amount).

Foreign transactions

A foreign exchange fee is usually charged on each transaction when you use your credit card abroad. A typical fee is 2.75 per cent so that there will be an extra cost of £11.00 when you pay a £400 hotel bill with your card.

Cash withdrawals are also expensive, with a withdrawal fee of 1.25 to 2 per cent and a minimum charge of £1.25 to £5. In addition, most credit cards start to charge interest from the day that you draw the cash, even if you pay your bill in full. There are some credit cards that allow you to put your card into credit before you leave so that you avoid paying interest.

Generally, if you're going abroad draw some cash before you go and take travellers cheques for further cash expenditure. Travellers cheques cost between 1 and 2 per cent in commission with a minimum charge of £3 or so.

How cashback works

The concept of cashback is similar to the idea behind loyalty cards in stores. Some cards give you back a bonus on what you spend (typically 0.5 to 1 per cent), which is credited to your account either monthly or annually. The idea, of course, is to encourage you to make all your credit card purchases on their card instead of someone else's. If you don't clear your balance each month, cashback still helps to pay off some of the interest on your borrowing.

The best cards for cashback depend on the amount you spend each year. For example, Nationwide offers 1 per cent for six months, whatever you spend, while Leeds & Holbeck and the Morgan Stanley Cashback and Platinum cards pay £10 if you spend £1,000 in a year. But you need to check your card's cashback rate regularly as they will change from time to time. Bear in mind also that some cards take away your right to cashback if you exceed your credit limit or pay late. However, cashback is unlikely to be the main factor determining your choice.

Choosing the best card for you

As we've seen, this isn't exactly a 'no brainer' but the summary of 17 selected cards in Table 3.1 may help you to make a choice if you pay three out of four bills on time (regular payer) or if, on average, you pay one in four bills on time (irregular payer). The table also shows which of these

Table 3.1 Selected credit cards

	Best For...*				Features		
	regular payer	irregular payer	never pay-off	0% deals	days to pay	APR (%)	penalty fee (£)
Abbey Flat Rate	–	–	*	–	28[a]	10.9	25[b]
Amex Gold	*	–	–		25	12.9	25
Bank of Ireland Moneyback MasterCard	*	*	–	–	20	14.9	15
Bank of Scotland One Visa	*	*	*	*	25	9.9[c]	25
Capital One No hassle MasterCard	–	*	*	–	26	6.9[c]	20
The Co-operative Bank Flat Rate Gold Visa	–	*	–	–	15	9.9[d]	25
The Co-operative Bank Flat Rate Platinum Visa	–	*	*	–	15	8.9[d]	25
The Co-operative Bank Platinum Tracker Visa	–	*	*	–	15	9.1	25
Halifax One Visa	–	–	*	*	25	9.9[c]	25
Halifax Platinum Balance Transfer Visa	–	–	–	*	25	10.5	25
Leeds & Holbeck MasterCard	–	*	*	–	26	16.9	20
More Than Cashback Rewards MasterCard	–	*	*	–	20	16.1[b]	20
Morgan Stanley Cashback MasterCard	–	*	–	–	26	17.9	20
Nationwide Cash Reward Visa	–	*	–	–	25	15.9	15
Northern Rock Base Rate Visa	–	–	*	*	25	13.9	15
Smile Visa	–	*	*	*	15	11.8[d]	15[e]
Virgin Flat Rate MasterCard	–	–	*	–	28[a]	10.9	25

Notes:
a   Up to 28 days.
b   First late payment fee refunded.
c   Typical rates. Actual rate depends on your circumstances.
d   9.9 per cent for Smile current account holders.
e   £15 for late payment. £20 for exceeding limit.

Source: Which?, December 2004

cards offer 0 per cent deals or a lower rate of interest for the first six months, their APR rates as of December 2004 and their penalty fees.

At that date, the best current deal identified by *Which?* was One Visa from Halifax/Bank of Scotland. They offered 0 per cent interest on balance transfers and new purchases for nine months and a typical APR rate after that of 9.9 per cent (more if you have a poor credit history).

Other good deals were on offer from HSBC with its Classic Card (standard rate 15.9 per cent) and HSBC Gold Card (standard rate 14.9 per cent). Both provided 0 per cent on balance transfers for nine months and 0 per cent on purchases until 1 September 2005. For more recent information, visit www.which.co.uk/creditcards.

Cautions

Most cards (not American Express) come with either the Visa or MasterCard logo, indicating that you can use them at all retail and service outlets that display the logo and which are part of one or both networks. In practice, most outlets accept either type of card. They are also useable for many transactions by mail, over the telephone, by fax or via the internet.

Minimum repayments

Credit card companies have steadily reduced the amount of repayment that you have to pay each month, over and above interest and other charges, from 5 to 3 or 2 per cent, and in some cases even less. If you pay only the minimum, it could take years to pay off your debt and, in the meantime, you will be paying heavy interest charges – often many times the value of the debt. As an example, with one reputable card offering a low rate of APR interest of 9.9 per cent, it would take you 14 years to pay off a £1,000 debt through minimum repayments only of 2 per cent.

Credit card cheques

Some credit card companies supply blank cheques on your credit card account as a temptation to spend more and many people receive cheques that they didn't ask for. Even if you pay your monthly bill in full, using such a cheque costs more than paying with your card because you are charged a handling fee of 2 per cent of the value of the cheque. Also, there's no right of claim, as there is with your credit card, when you order goods that don't arrive or are faulty. So, don't use them.

Risk-based interest charges

The current Consumer Credit Act requires that companies now have to say 'typical' against the quoted APR interest in all their publicity material, even if all applicants are offered that rate. If the rate actually offered depends on your credit status it will have to say so.

Charging an interest rate dependent on your credit rating is known as risk-based pricing (RBP) and is used more and more by both credit card and loan companies.

Credit reference agencies

There are three main credit reference agencies (CRAs): Equifax, Experian and Callcredit. Lenders are supposed to use CRAs to make sure that they are lending more money only to people who can afford to make repayments, but none of the three CRAs holds complete information on the credit files of all card companies and other lenders.

Credit card companies have now signed up to an agreement, embodied in a new Bill passing through Parliament, which says they will share as much information with CRAs as they are allowed to by law. It is uncertain how much historic information will be held on file. This improvement may not be to your advantage if any of the information recorded on your file is inaccurate and out of date, as it could mean that you are refused credit unfairly. You do have a right to a copy of your credit file from any of the three CRAs for a fee of £2 a time. Their contact details are:

Callcredit: www.callcredit.plc.uk (0870 060 1414)
Equifax: www.equifax.co.uk (08705 143700)
Experian: www.experian.co.uk (0870 241 6212)

However, be warned from experience that it is extremely difficult to have any incorrect data removed from your file.

Perhaps the last word

Several years ago Matt Barrett, then Chief Executive of Barclays Bank and now Chairman, gave evidence to a House of Commons Select Committee investigating the credit industry. When asked whether he used any of the Barclaycard products his reply was that they were much too expensive for him! As they say, there's no answer to that.

The conclusion of this chapter, therefore, is that repayment of some or all of your credit card debt is a very good way of using your windfall and saving money. You will save more in interest and card charges than you can earn on interest on any bank deposit or savings account

Checklist

1. You can't compare credit card interest rates directly because they calculate charges in different ways. For current interest APRs check www.which.co.uk/creditcards regularly.

2. Be sure that you understand what is the interest-free period on each card. The actual length of time in which you have to pay from receipt of your bill varies from 25 days down to 14 days or less, if the card company doesn't mail its statements on the statement date.

3. 0 per cent interest offers to new card users may apply to new purchases or to balances transferred from another credit card, or both. Take care that there is no separate commission charge on accepting a transferred balance.

4. If a card gives you 0 per cent interest on your transferred balance but charges interest on new purchases, it will probably use your repayments to pay off the lowest rate debt first (that is, the transferred balance).

5. The best way to avoid late payment charges is to set up a monthly direct debit, at least for the minimum payment. Several card companies don't charge a penalty the first time you pay late. Nearly all cards charge a penalty for exceeding the credit limit.

6. Using your credit card abroad costs more with a fee on each transaction. Take some cash and travellers cheques, which are cheaper.

7. Cashbacks are credits to your card of a bonus as a percentage of your total expenditure. Nice to have, but not a major factor in choosing your credit card.

8. Use Table 3.1, the terms of selected credit cards, as a guide to help you choose your card.

9. Never use the cheques supplied without request by your credit card company and don't tempt yourself by asking for them.
10. To pay off your credit card debt in a reasonable period of time, make much more than the minimum payments each month. If you have the cash, it is better to pay off the whole balance on the most expensive card than a bit off each.

Better borrowing – overdrafts and personal loans

If your windfall or any increase in income isn't enough to pay off your deferred payment deal (before interest is chargeable) or your expensive credit card balance, there is another way that you can improve your finances and save interest. You can take out a bank overdraft or personal loan at a much cheaper rate of interest.

In this chapter, we'll examine each alternative before we move on in Part 3 to earning money on surplus cash after your expensive debt has been repaid. I haven't included a section on secured loans or mortgages because this is borrowing of a different kind, often involving other members of the family and certainly affecting family security.

Bank overdrafts

An overdraft is not the cheapest but is the most flexible form of debt. It is important to understand your bank's attitude to giving you credit in this way before you ask for one. An overdraft is simply an arrangement to allow you to draw on your current account beyond the funds that are there at any one time up to a certain limit. The bank will view your overdraft as a facility to help you manage your cash flow in the intervals between receipt of income.

If you are employed and receive a regular salary cheque or, more likely these days, a direct transfer from your employer into your account at the month-end, your bank may very well allow you to 'overdraw' up to the amount of one month's salary or a bit more. If you are self-employed and the receipt of income from your customers or clients is more erratic, the bank may allow you rather more if you can show that there has been a constant average inflow over a period of time.

Bank managers today have very little discretion, which means that it is less important whether your bank manager likes your face or not – perhaps a good thing! If you visit your local high street bank to ask for an overdraft you will find that he/she inputs the information you give into a PC, which gives a head office response according to a mathematical formula. Some banks give you an automatic £500 or £1000 overdraft limit when you open a current account, but let's assume that you are asking for rather more than that.

All overdrafts are reviewed formally at regular intervals, typically six months or a year, but the bank has the right to withdraw the 'facility' at any time and to demand repayment. What the bank will want to see in the conduct of your account is a fluctuating balance – hopefully, that the account is in credit immediately after your salary arrives and that the debit balance stays within the overdraft limit throughout the month following. If the debit balance remains solidly at or close to the overdraft limit for an extended period, the bank will judge that your debt is solid and almost certainly propose that the overdraft is converted into an unsecured loan. We'll come to that later in this chapter.

Which bank?

There are several quite different aspects of personal banking for you to consider: overdraft interest rates, unsecured loan terms and availability, current account management fees and transaction charges, interest on credit balances and deposit accounts and other services such as telephone and internet banking.

For now, we are most interested in the first three elements and your initial list of possible banks will probably be based on the four major high street banks that used to be known as 'clearing banks': Barclays Bank, HSBC, Lloyds TSB and NatWest, which is now a part of Royal Bank of Scotland (RBS). There is also RBS itself and Bank of Scotland with branch networks extending to England, and some other accredited banks such as Clydesdale and the Co-operative Bank and a number of building societies that now offer personal banking services.

Among the building societies are Abbey, Alliance & Leicester, Halifax, Woolwich and Yorkshire Banks. And, if you are happy to bank remotely by telephone or on the internet there is a newer generation of banks offering full banking services that includes First Direct (an offshoot of HSBC), Nationwide, Cahoot, Intelligent Finance and Smile. If you are looking for an overdraft facility, the terms highlighted here will hopefully help you to choose the bank that suits you best.

Interest

HSBC, the United Kingdom's largest high street bank, charges currently an estimated annual rate (EAR) of 14.8 per cent and, in its 'January Sales' promotion valid up to 31 January 2005, offered nine months interest-free credit on approved overdrafts to new customers.

In September 2004 the overdraft EARs of other banks varied from 6.57 per cent (Nationwide), through 8.29 per cent (Clydesdale Bank and Yorkshire Bank) up to 18.9 per cent (Bank of Scotland and Halifax) with Co-operative Bank the most expensive at 19.56 per cent. Among the 'big four', HSBC was the cheapest except for Barclays Bank Platinum Banking and Bank of Scotland Extra customers.

Of course, if you are using your overdraft as the bank intends, the actual amount by which you are overdrawn will vary throughout the month, so that the interest charges in £s will be less than the EAR rate times the amount of the overdraft limit because the bank charges according to usage. As an example, if you were to use an authorized £1,000 overdraft with an EAR of 14.8 per cent at that level for two weeks in every month, you might pay interest of as little as £64 a year.

However, as with credit cards, the interest charges are only one part of the total cost, particularly if you misuse your overdraft.

Monthly charges and arrangement fees

One or two banks still charge a monthly overdraft fee, and rather more charge arrangement fees, typically 1.25 to 2 per cent of the overdraft limit if it is more than a specified amount. You need to take these charges into account when comparing interest charges before you choose your bank.

Unauthorized overdraft interest and charges

If you expect to go over the top of your overdraft limit occasionally, this is where current account banking becomes really expensive. Unauthorized overdraft charges and their application really 'sort the sheep from the goats' when making your choice of bank.

Most banks charge a much higher rate of interest on amounts over the approved overdraft limit. Among the Big Four only HSBC charges the same rate. Some of the banks that offer the more reasonable rates of interest on approved overdrafts (including two of those named above) charge their higher unauthorized rates on the whole amount overdrawn including the part that is within the agreed limit.

Penalty fees for going 'over the top' can be even more expensive. Some banks charge fees (typically £25 or £30) for every transaction such as a direct debit, standing order or cheque over your limit, even if payment isn't made or reversed. Others charge daily or monthly fees or a single fee for exceeding your overdraft limit instead of a charge for each transaction.

Some banks automatically supply small buffers above their overdraft limits, say £10 or £50 or ignore the overrun before they make charges for those who exceed their facilities occasionally (for example, once in six months). After that, you will be charged every time as soon as you go a penny above your limit.

An extreme case, experienced recently with one of the Big Four banks, occurred when a customer whose account balance was just within her overdraft limit was allowed to draw a small cash amount on her debit card at an ATM (automated teller machine, commonly known as a 'cashpoint machine'), which took her just £3 over the limit and was promptly charged a penalty fee of £25. So, take care; you have been warned!

Managing your overdraft

It will be clear to you that if you are going to use an overdraft, you must try to stay within the approved limit. If you don't, the cost of running your account will very likely exceed the cost of any more expensive debt that you are replacing. An obvious point is to negotiate an overdraft limit that you are confident of keeping within. Anticipating the second part of this chapter, you may decide that it is better to have a personal loan together with a smaller overdraft.

Overdraft management is possibly the best argument for using internet banking, which is very simple if you have a personal computer (PC). Using your password and personal code that your bank will provide, you can check daily the state of your current account and all recent transactions. You can see what cheques are not yet presented before you sign any more cheques or withdraw cash. If you find that you are likely to go over the limit, you will also be able to make a transfer from any other bank or savings account that you may have to cover the position.

It's easy to forget bank charges and interest, any direct debits (DDs) and standing orders (SOs) that may hit your account before your next salary transfer or other credit arrives. I find it helpful to keep by me a list of all DDs and SOs with the dates in the month when they are usually debited and the date when my bank debits its interest and charges, with a note of what I expect them to be. Even this is not foolproof and you may still make a mistake in your calculations. If you do find that you are almost certainly going to exceed your overdraft limit, the best thing to do is to call your bank and talk through the alternative actions you can take. If you don't do this too often, you will probably find your bank helpful. They may give you a temporary or even permanent increase of your limit.

Unsecured personal loans

Generally, an unsecured personal loan from your bank is the cheapest way to borrow larger sums of money. Personal loans that are unsecured are usually available for amounts from £1,000 up to £25,000. Also, unlike overdrafts, the interest rate is fixed so that you know exactly what you are going to pay each month.

Banks usually require monthly repayment by direct debit and there is often a penalty for early repayment. The actual interest rate that you are offered will probably depend on your credit score when a similar routine to that described in agreeing the terms of an overdraft is carried out by the bank.

Comparative deals

In November 2004, *Which?* carried out a survey of 100 companies to find out their unsecured personal loan terms. Their top 11 list of 'Best Buys' contained some surprises and did not include any of the Big Four banks. For a £10,000 loan repayable over five years the APR interest rates among the top 11 varied from 5.7 per cent to 6.9 per cent.

Among the cheaper deals at 6.10 APR each were the AA and Sainsbury's Bank, but both of these are available only on internet banking. Three building societies were also rated highly: Abbey (5.8 per cent); Alliance & Leicester (5.9 per cent) and Nationwide (6.7 per cent). The lowest APR (6.0 per cent) was on offer from Smile, another loan provider via the internet only.

The HSBC January 2005 promotion also included a special offer on personal loans for which its normal APR was 9.9 per cent. The discounted rate, available only up to the end of January, was 7.7 per cent for loans of £10,000 to £14,990 and 7.1 per cent for loans of £15,000 or more. On these terms, a £10,000 loan repayable over five years would require monthly repayments of £200.99 and a £20,000 loan would involve payments of £394.89 each month. However, the table providing examples of HSBC terms also quoted alternative 'with protection' terms, which introduces you to another minefield where you will need to tread carefully.

Payment protection insurance

The object of payment protection insurance is to pay off your loan account debt if you are unable to work. That sounds like a good idea but it doesn't work if you are self-employed or working on contract. PPI is expensive and also gives limited cover only.

In the HSBC special offer quoted above, the PPI premiums would add £43.61 (21.7 per cent) to the monthly cost of a £10,000 personal loan and £84.11 extra (21.3 per cent) to the cost of a £20,000 loan. Over the five-year period in the examples, PPI would add £2,616.60 to the total cost of the £10,000 loan and £5,046.60 to the cost of borrowing £20,000. Almost certainly, you'll do better taking out an income protection policy with an insurance company, that will give you money to use how you will and is not tied to the personal loan. Alternatively, if you think that the chances of being able to make a claim really are remote, you could simply save the money.

In its special offer, HSBC was careful to show the 'with protection' and 'without protection' premiums separately, but not all loan providers are so scrupulous. Some include PPI in their quotes and, worse still, some neglect to tell you that PPI is included. This is another area where future legislation will hopefully ban bad selling practices.

It has been calculated that, by selling PPI with their loans, personal loan companies make at least £1 billion a year in commission. You won't be surprised that credit card companies also sell PPI and that premiums are usually added to your credit card balance so that you are charged interest on the increased debt. Here, you are definitely better off not buying the PPI cover because it will pay off only a small proportion of your debt each month if you are not working.

Checklist

1. An overdraft is the most flexible but not the cheapest form of debt. Your bank will only allow you an overdraft on application within its credit formula, typically one month's income or a bit more.
2. If your account remains solidly near or at the overdraft limit, expect your bank to ask you to replace the overdraft arrangement with an unsecured personal loan.
3. Estimated annual interest rates (EAR) on overdrafts can vary from 6.57 per cent up to 19.56 per cent. If you were to use a £1,000 overdraft at an EAR of 14.8 per cent up to that level for two weeks a month, your annual interest charge might be no more than £64.
4. When comparing bank interest charges on overdrafts take into account any arrangement or monthly fees that a bank might charge.
5. Keep within your overdraft limit to avoid paying higher rates of interest on amounts above (sometimes charged on the whole amount of the debt once you are over the top) penalty fees of £25 or £30 per transaction whether or not payment is made.
6. Use internet banking services to manage your current account within your overdraft limit. Don't forget DDs, SOs and bank interest and charges when budgeting ahead.
7. If you think you're going to be over the top, talk to your bank before it happens.
8. Personal unsecured loans are available, usually from £1,000 to £25,000. The interest rate is fixed and you make monthly payments by DD.
9. The actual interest rate will depend on your credit score. APR rates vary from a minimum of 5.8 per cent upwards (more from the Big Four high street banks). A £10,000 loan at 7.7 per cent APR repayable over five years will cost you £200.99 each month.
10. Beware of payment protection insurance (PPI), which lenders offer for an additional monthly charge. PPI is expensive, gives limited cover only and does not apply if you are self-employed or work on contract. An income protection policy with an insurance company is a better bet.

Part Three
Passive saving

5 Saving for a rainy day

So far we've thought about saving money through wise spending, better borrowing and using your surplus cash to reduce expensive debt. These are 'savings' but not quite the same as actual 'saving', you will say – and, of course, you're quite right.

Most of us think of saving as essentially putting cash aside to save up for some future purchase – next year's holiday, perhaps – or to build up an emergency sum 'for a rainy day' or a crisis, such as urgent repairs to your house or car. The requirements for this kind of saving, in order of importance, are to:

- put the cash somewhere safe;
- have rapid access to it;
- maintain its value;
- earn some income.

There are a number of different ways in which you can do this, and I have called them collectively 'passive saving'. Why passive? Because once you have chosen where to put your money, you don't need to do anything more until you come to draw the cash. Unless, of course, you find somewhere better to put it and decide to switch.

In praise of cash

Basically, cash is something you keep in your pocket to spend each day or over the coming week. That is not a way of saving money; if you're like me, cash in the pocket or purse has an amazing way of evaporating almost instantly! We know too that, when inflation is high, unspent cash will buy progressively less and less.

For the same reason, you know that hoarding your cash in banknotes under the mattress (or in the teapot you never use on the top shelf of the kitchen cabinet) will not protect its value. There is the added risk of loss through break-in and theft. However, if you deposit your cash with a bank, building society, some other financial institution or the post office your money will be safe and you may be able to earn interest on it.

Deposit accounts

If you want to be able to withdraw all or a part of your money from a deposit account instantly, the interest rate you receive will be low. If you are willing to give notice of withdrawal, say, several weeks or months, higher interest rates will be available. The interest rate may also be better if you are prepared to conduct all your transactions through the post, on the telephone or via the internet. In Table 5.1 you will find a few examples of recent interest rates offered. Building societies tend to offer better rates than high street banks. You may feel uncomfortable in depositing your money with lesser known banks that offer even higher rates of interest.

Table 5.1 shows that as of 20 March 2005, if you had £100 to deposit, you could earn 5.0 per cent on instant access with ING Direct (a major

Table 5.1 Deposit account interest rates – a selection of best rates at 20 March 2005

£	Instant access	Up to 90 days' notice	12 months' notice
100	ING Direct ING Direct Savings 5.00% [PT]	Scottish Widows Bk 60-day notice 4.77% [BPT]	Halifax Bank Regular saver 7.07% [FP]
1,000	The AA AA Tel. Savings 5.26% [BDT]	Chelsea BS Call-direct 70 5.20% [BPT]	Julian Hodge Bk 1-year Fixed 5.4% [F]
5,000	The AA AA Tel. Savings 5.26% [BDT]	Chelsea BS Call-direct 70 5.20% [BPT]	Sabanci Bank 1-year Fixed 5.51% [F]
10,000 plus	The AA AA Tel. Savings 5.26% [BDT]	Chelsea BS Call-direct 70 5.20% [BPT]	Sabanci Bank 1-year Fixed 5.51% [F]

Notes:
B – Rate cited includes bonus.
D – Deposit taker is Birmingham Midshires.
F – Fixed interest.
P – Postal Account.
T – Telephone Account.

Source: The Mail on Sunday 20 Feb. 2005

Netherlands bank) on a postal and telephone account or, if you deposited £1,000, the AA Bank would offer you 5.26 per cent on its telephone savings account. In fact, the best rate available in both cases was from Alliance & Leicester's No-Notice Online Saver Account at 5.35 per cent available only on the internet (not shown in the table).

If you were prepared to give up to 90 days' notice, the best rate (including bonus) on a £100 deposit was 4.77 per cent from Scottish Widows Bank for a postal and telephone services account. For a deposit of £1,000 Chelsea Building Society offered a straight 5.2 per cent on the same basis. You will note that the rates offered on a £1,000 deposit are higher than those on £100 and higher still if placed on 12 months' notice.

In order to get the best deal, you need to check interest rates regularly. They are posted in the daily Press. One particularly useful source is personal finance section of *The Mail on Sunday*, which includes its own 'Stats Station' from which Table 5.1 is taken.

The value of your money will grow faster if you leave the interest earned in your account so that it accumulates yet more interest on the increased sum on deposit. However, there are two external factors beyond your control that will reduce the value of your deposit: inflation (which is unavoidable) and income tax.

Foreign currency deposits

One more form of deposit account that you might want to consider, if you travel to certain countries regularly or have a home abroad and need to move funds regularly, is a foreign currency savings account. These accounts are available either in the form of instant access or fixed-term deposits. Of course, an account in euros will be useful if you holiday abroad in any of the eurozone countries. The high street banks and some others will offer you this facility if you ask.

Inflation

I've already referred to the impact of inflation in the Introduction, and this is as good a moment as any to discuss it more fully. There is an inflation effect on the value of all savings and also on investments when we come to them in Part 4. In the last 30 years, inflation has been as high as 15 per cent per year although it has been held down to less than 2 per cent since 2001. Over the longer term it is easier to think of inflation in terms of the familiar products that we buy daily. For example, over the span of the last century, a pint of milk that cost 8p in 1900 had risen to 25p by 1999, while the price of a dozen eggs rose from 6.9p to £1.57. The price of a daily newspaper, which was 35p in 1999, had risen from 1.2p while a first-class stamp was 26p, up from 0.4p in 1900.

We can define inflation in a variety of different ways: as the rise in the prices of only the goods and services that you purchase yourself or as the overall increase in the price of goods and services across the economy as a whole. Some consumer price statistics separate the rise in the price of housing from price rises on other items of consumer expenditure. No doubt, if you were a member of a religious order living on a remote island off the cost of Scotland, the impact of inflation would be different, as would your expenditure pattern from what it is now, but let's assume that we are 'average' UK consumers. Therefore, we need to relate interest on savings to the standard measurement, known as the 'Consumer Price Index' (CPI for short).

In his chapter on cash (*Handbook of Personal Wealth Management*, 2005 Kogan Page, London) John Dawe, research department manager of the Private Banking division of Lloyds TSB, puts inflation into perspective:

> Would you rather earn 15 per cent interest per annum on your cash when inflation is at 20 per cent, or 3 per cent interest when inflation is at 1 per cent? A 15 per cent return looks enticing but the second proposition is actually more worthwhile as under the first, your money will be able to buy less and less each year.

Let's look at a real life example of a bank deposit. In December 2001, I had a small amount on deposit with Scottish Widows Bank. There have been no withdrawals and, during the three-year period to December 2004 a modest amount of interest had accumulated. Table 5.2 calculates the inflation effect at the recent low levels of inflation. In the final column, we show what the 'real value' of the deposit would have been at December 2004, if the rather higher rates of CPI between 1996 and 1998 had occurred.

You will see that the value of my deposit, in terms of purchasing power, was £130.05 at December 2004, an increase of 8.76 per cent over three years. Under the rather higher inflation conditions the end value would have been £120.84, an increase of just 1.06 per cent after actually losing value in the first of the two intermediary years. You can work out for yourself by how much the value would have diminished had CPI been at 5 per cent throughout the three-year period (answer at the end of the chapter*).

Table 5.2 Interest earned before and after inflation on deposit

Year end (Dec)	Deposit plus interest net	Inflation CPI actual	Current value £	Inflation CPI 1996–98	Adjusted value £
2001	119.57	–	–		119.57
2002	122.97	1.3	121.37	3.2	119.03
2003	126.15	1.3	122.93	2.5	119.15
2004	130.05	1.8	124.55	1.8	120.84

Source: Scottish Widows VIP Premier Account and published inflation rates

Income tax

Interest on bank deposit accounts is normally credited to your account net of income tax at the standard rate so that taxation has already been taken into account if you are a basic rate tax payer. The current levels of taxable income for the year ending 5 April 2006 are:

■ The first £2,090 (after deduction of personal allowances) is taxed at 10 per cent.
■ The next £30,310 is taxed at 22 per cent (the 'basic rate') on earned income and 20 per cent on savings.
■ Anything above is taxed at 40 per cent.

It follows that, if you are not paying the basic rate, you will be able to reclaim a tax refund. On the other hand, if you are at the 40 per cent rate you should pay additional tax on bank interest received, which is treated as income at the higher level.

There are forms of savings and investment where there is tax relief either on your contributions or on the income or capital gain. We shall look at these in the next chapter and also in Parts 4 and 5. There are also ISAs, which can be a form of passive saving and are discussed below.

Regular savings accounts

Within my definition of passive saving, you may also consider putting your money into types of account other than a simple deposit account. The first of these is a regular savings account where you contract to pay a minimum amount each month into the account for a minimum period of time ('the term'). Some accounts allow you to miss occasional monthly payments and some allow an occasional withdrawal without forfeiting the bonus element.

Budgeting

Before opening a regular savings account, you need to be sure that you can maintain the regular deposits to which you commit yourself. Therefore, a permanent increase in income rather than a one-off windfall is a better reason to open a regular savings account. Even then, you should check the family budget carefully – not just income and expenditure but the cash flow as well, since timing is crucial when you make this kind of commitment.

If you haven't made a formal budget recently, you may find the budget calculator on the www.fsa.gov.uk/consumer website with the accompanying notes on where to find information about your income and spending useful. In order to use it as a cash flow calculator, just add a column for each week or month in which you enter the actual cash amounts coming in and going out. You may also want to include more detailed items of expenditure. For example, the FSA calculator doesn't include holidays or bank charges.

Comparative interest rates

Personal savings accounts, with the bonus element included, offer better rates of interest than deposit accounts, and *Which?* February 2005 issue selected two banks and seven building societies that it considered to be 'best buys'. This information is reproduced in Table 5.3. As well as the interest rates it shows the minimum and maximum deposit that you may make each month, whether or not you may make extra deposits, how many times you may make a withdrawal without penalty and the term.

If you are prepared to sign up for a one-year term, the two best deals are from Abbey Bank and Halifax/Bank of Scotland, each offering 6.5 per cent and 6 per cent respectively. The only difference lies in the minimum and maximum monthly deposits allowed.

As with plain deposit accounts, you should check comparative rates regularly. The Banking Code, a voluntary code of good practice by which all deposit takers claim to abide, says that banks must inform you if savings rates have not gone up in line with base lending rates when they rise, and must then give you the option of withdrawing or transferring

Table 5.3   Regular savings accounts – selected deals at November 2005 on £100 to £2,500

	Interest %	Deposits (£) min	max	Extra payments allowed	Withdrawals	Term years
Abbey	6.50	20	500	No	0	1
Bath BS	5.35	10	200	No	1	3
Cheshire BS	5.75	25	250	No	1	–
Derbyshire BS	5.85	10	1,000	Yes	1	–
Furness BS	5.65	50	200	Yes	0	5
Halifax/Bank Scotland	6.00	25	250	No	0	1
Hanley Econ. BS	5.45	25	1,000	No	1	–
Leeds & Holbeck BS	5.50	20	500	Yes	1	–
Yorkshire BS	5.85	10	100	No	0	3

Source: Which? magazine

your money without penalty. However, banks with low savings rates, where customer expectations are not high, can get away with not notifying their depositors, while banks with higher rates have to notify. In any case, it's a good idea to consult www.which.co.uk/whichextra or the financial pages of the national Press regularly.

ISAs

Individual Savings Accounts (ISAs) replaced both Tax Exempt Special Savings Accounts (TESSAs) and Personal Equity Plans (PEPs) in April 1999. The last TESSA came to an end on 5 April 2004. The thousands of investors who took out a Tessa in 1999 were given six months after that date to roll the cash into a TESSA Only Isa and keep the tax-free benefits. Existing PEPs were unaffected by the change but no new ones could be opened.

Generally, anyone resident in the United Kingdom for tax purposes who is 18 and over can open an ISA in either of its two forms: the Mini ISA and the Maxi ISA. Those who are 16 or 17 years old may open a Cash Mini ISA. The Financial Services Authority (FSA) describes an ISA as a 'wrapper' in which you can place your savings. Through the FSA, the government has set charges, access and terms standards know as 'CATs' to which all ISA providers are required to conform. The CAT Standards are very clear:

▌ *Charges* No one-off or regular charges except in prescribed circumstances, for example, duplicate statements.

▌ *Access* Minimum deposits no more than £10. Withdrawals available within seven working days.

▌ *Terms* Interest rates no lower than 2 per cent below the Bank of England base rate.

The main attraction of ISAs is that, within the investment limits that are set by the government, all your returns made by investments in ISAs are tax-free.

The investment limits apply to your total contributions during the tax year, not the balance of your ISA so that your savings can accumulate nicely. You cannot subscribe in the same tax year to a Mini ISA and a Maxi ISA, more than one Mini ISA of the same type, or more than one Maxi ISA.

Mini ISA

You may invest in one of the two following components in each of your Mini ISAs: cash (bank and building society savings accounts, National Savings & Investments); or stocks and shares unit trusts, shares, bonds, and so on). They can be held with the same or different providers. Currently, the maximum investment amount each tax year is £3,000 cash and £4,000 stocks and shares (increased from £3,000 as of 6 April 2005). You may open one Mini ISA of each type in a tax year.

Maxi ISA

You could include the same elements of cash or stocks and shares in your Maxi ISA within one account and with the same provider. The maximum investment amount is currently £7,000 in each tax year, which can be entirely in stocks and shares or up to £3,000 in cash. There are two further ground rules: your Maxi ISA must have a stocks and shares component and you are only allowed to open one Maxi ISA in any one tax year.

Tax benefits

ISAs are free of income tax. You do not have to pay tax on interest, dividends, or bonuses received from your ISAs. If your ISA increases in value, you make a capital gain but that is free of tax too. You don't have to pay capital gains tax (CGT) but ISAs are not exempt from inheritance tax (IHT).

Choosing a Cash Mini ISA

There is a wide variety of ISA savings accounts available to you, which pay interest gross without deducting income tax. Up-to-date details of most of them are provided in the Consumer Information section on the FSA website in its comparative tables: www.fsa.gov.uk/tables.

If you enter the notice period that you are prepared to give on withdrawals, the amount you intend to save initially and the amount you intend to deposit regularly, you can call up a list of the products that satisfy your requirements. For example, if on 17 February 2005, you had chosen to compare products with interest earned on a tax-free basis, with no notice of withdrawal and with an initial saving of £100 and regular deposits afterwards, your FSA table would have shown 82 products in alphabetical order. Six of the accounts identified offered interest rates of 5.00 per cent or more. You would have found the highest rates with the Alliance & Leicester (5.40 per cent), Abbey (5.35 per cent) and Yorkshire Building Society (5.20 per cent). The Yorkshire account is available only via the internet, Alliance & Leicester can be opened at a branch or by post and accessed by telephone or the internet, and Abbey, which you can also open at a branch or by post, can only be accessed by post.

Other forms of ISA investment

For this chapter, which is about passive savings only – not investments – we have considered Cash Mini ISAs. Investment in stocks and shares through an ISA has the same risks as any investment in stocks and shares. The price of shares can go down as well as up and it is possible that the value will fall below the original investment. This could also happen if you hold overseas securities as a result of changes in the rate of exchange. We'll discuss stocks and shares in Part 4 – Financial Investment.

The same sort of argument applies to some investment-type life assurance products. They used to be considered 'safe as houses' but in recent years some products, particularly in endowment assurance, have proved to be conspicuously unsafe. Mis-selling, imprudent management and errors of calculation by actuaries have caused the downfall of several well-known companies and also pension funds. (Actuaries are the experts who compile and analyse statistics in relation to life expectancy and therefore the likely incidence of claims under life insurance policies among other kinds of risk.)

Checklist

1. Hoarding your cash in banknotes will not protect its value. A deposit account is safer.
2. If you want instant withdrawal from a deposit account, the interest paid will be low. Higher interest rates may be available on accounts where notice of several weeks or months has to be given. Some higher rate accounts are available if you conduct all your transactions through the post, on the telephone or via the internet.
3. Check interest rates regularly to get the best deal. Current rates are quoted in the national daily Press, the Consumer Information section on the FSA website (www.fsa.gov.uk) or the *Which?* website (www.which.co.uk).
4. Foreign currency deposit accounts may be useful if you take holidays abroad or have a home abroad.
5. The value of your money will grow faster if you leave the interest earned in your account to accumulate. However, the amount on deposit will be reduced in value by inflation. If the rate of inflation is greater than the interest rate you receive, the value of your deposit will decrease over time.
6. Income tax at the basic rate of 20 per cent is deducted from the interest credited to your deposit account. Currently, if your annual income is less than £6,985 you will be able to claim some tax back. If your income is above £37,295 you may have to pay more tax on your interest received.
7. Regular savings accounts where you contract to pay a minimum amount each month into the account for a minimum period of time offer better rates of interest than deposit accounts but the number of withdrawals allowed is very often limited. Check comparative rates regularly from the same information sources.
8. Individual Savings Accounts (ISAs) are available to any UK tax resident over the age of 18 in either of two forms: Mini ISAs and Maxi ISAs – 16- and 17-year-olds may open a Cash Mini ISA. You cannot subscribe in the same year for a Mini ISA and a Maxi ISA.
9. ISAs are free of income tax and ISA savings accounts pay interest gross. You do not have to pay tax on interest, dividends or

bonuses received from your ISAs. You don't pay capital gains tax (CGT) on gains but ISAs are not exempt from inheritance tax (IHT).

10. The maximum investment amount allowed each tax year in Mini ISAs is currently £3,000 cash plus £1,000 life insurance and £4,000 in stocks and shares. Maxi ISAs must have a stocks and shares component (up to £7,000 in each tax year). You may also invest up to £3,000 of your Maxi ISA in cash. Again, the number of withdrawals allowed is very often limited.

*With inflation at 5 per cent each year the 'real' value of the original sum on deposit of £119.57 in the example plus accumulated interest (Table 5.2) would have shrunk to just £112 after three years.

A UNIQUE APPROACH TO PRIVATE MEDICAL INSURANCE

PruHealth is a totally new kind of Private Medical Insurance provider. Whilst it provides the type of quality cover you'd expect from any leading provider, the difference is, you can manage the cost of your premiums.

Save up to 30% straightaway

If you haven't needed to make a claim in the last 3 years, you'll save up to 30% immediately, just by answering a few simple questions. And if you don't need to claim in any given year, you'll get 25% back to put towards the next year's premium.

Pay even less, just by staying healthy

PruHealth believe that if you're looking after yourself, your health cover costs should fall. That's why with PruHealth, if you're making an effort – for example, by eating sensibly or getting some exercise – you could get even more of next year's premium back. That could be as much as 100%.

Innovation but not at the expense of quality cover

Whilst PruHealth are committed to reducing the cost of health insurance there's no compromise on the quality of the cover on offer.

You can choose from a range of plans, from the essentials to what they believe is amongst the most comprehensive you'll find. Each is designed to provide the best cover available at a price that's right for you.

You'll also have the reassurance of access to:

- over 450 private hospitals and screening centres nationwide,
- 16,000 specialist private consultants within all areas of medicine
- Assigned nurse case managers to help with long term treatments

Call 0800 092 6666 now to see how much you can save

For an immediate personal quote and information pack, call today, quoting ref PR001, and find out how you can benefit from becoming a PruHealth member. You can also find out more information by visiting **www.pruhealth.co.uk**

6 Saving for the future

The last chapter discussed some of the ways that you can save your money safely and still have either instant or quite ready access to use it. Let's move on now to more serious saving for the future where you start to save with the intention of adding to the sum saved over a considerable period of time. Savings of this kind are not intended for use as emergency funds in the event of crisis.

Child Trust Funds

In January 2005, the government introduced a new savings scheme for children born after 1 September 2002, called the Child Trust Fund (CTF). If you have a child who is eligible, you may claim a benefit from the government, which will normally make an initial payment, via a voucher, of £250 (£500 for low income families and children in care). This money, and all further contributions that you may make, will be placed into a special CTF account until the child reaches the age of 18. Key points on CTFs:

▊ The CTF belongs to the child and all contributions will be a gift to them.
▊ Family and friends can add up to £1,200 per birthday year to the CTF by a single lump sum or regular payments.
▊ Money cannot be taken out of a CTF until the child reaches the age of 18.
▊ At 18, the money will be free from income and capital gains tax.
▊ An annual statement will be sent giving the value of the CTF and full details of all transactions.

The sooner you open an account, the sooner the money will start to grow for your child. If you don't open an account within 12 months, the Inland

Revenue will open a stakeholder account for your child. Provided that you are the registered contact, you can move this account to another provider. The new provider will inform the Inland Revenue about the change so that your child's records are kept up to date. The Inland Revenue makes no charge but there may be a charge by the provider for the costs of transferring the account or, if it is necessary, to buy or sell investments.

The FSA website, www.childtrustfund.gov.uk, identifies a list of providers that have notified the Inland Revenue that they will distribute CTF accounts. The list is updated daily but it is not guaranteed that any provider will manage a CTF satisfactorily or that that any account is approved. On 22 February 2005, there were 50 banks, building societies and other organizations on the list.

Savings for children ineligible for CTFs

If you are a parent and you give money to your child outside the CTF scheme and it produces more than £100 a year income, that income will be taxed as if it is yours and not your child's. However, there are some savings products designed especially for children where the income is not treated as the parent's income. For example, the National Savings & Investments (NS&I) children's bonus bonds that can be purchased for any child under 16 earn tax-free income. The following are just some of the main ways of investing for children:

Savings accounts

Banks and building societies offer special cash deposit accounts for young people and children. In most cases, parents can arrange for children to get the interest on their children's savings without the tax being taken off by completing Inland Revenue form R85.

Local building society accounts tend to pay higher rates of interest but you have to live in the area. In the December 2004 edition of its magazine, *Which?* identified seven building societies and two banks offering accounts with minimum deposits of £10 where interest of 5.00 per cent up to 5.50 per cent was payable. Two of them could be held open up to the age of 21, but the two offering the highest rates (Alliance & Leicester and Saffron Walden Building Society) have maximum age limits of 16.

Individual Savings Accounts (ISAs)

We've been here before in the last chapter. At the age of 16, young people can have a Cash ISA in their own right with the same subscription rights as for adults. Until they are 18 they cannot hold investments in an ISA themselves, but you could use your ISA to save for them.

Friendly Societies

A Friendly Society is a mutual organization in which the people who have investments are members. Their savings and investment products are attractive because they can offer tax-free savings products for children, which allow you to save £300 a year tax-free. Like CTFs, the parent is not taxable on income from the investment in a Friendly Society product. Adults can also save up to £300 a year tax-free.

National Savings

National Savings & Investments products are backed by the government and all capital invested is 100 per cent guaranteed. Some NS&I products are particularly suitable for children. We go into the details of their various products in the next section where we look at longer-term savings for adults. All their products can be found on the website: www.nationalsavings.co.uk.

Investment funds

In an investment fund your money is pooled with other people's money and invested in a wide range of shares in companies. You make money if the companies do well when the value of the shares go up. Of course, if the value of the shares goes down you can also lose money.

Your child cannot invest money in stocks and shares, but you can invest for them in the form of a trust or add the child's name to the account holder name. We'll have a closer look at investment funds in Part 4.

National Savings & Investments

All NS&I products are 'deposit-based'. You can always get back the money you paid in, plus accumulated interest. They make an excellent home for your savings if you don't want to take risks. Before deciding where to save or invest you will want to compare NS&I terms with those of similar deposit-based products from banks and building societies that are also considered safe.

NS&I in tax-free savings

You can invest up to a total of £93,000 tax-free in various NS&I bonds and savings accounts:

■ *Cash Mini ISA* Save from £10 up to £3,000 in the 2005/06 tax year.
■ *Index-linked savings certificates* Returns are guaranteed to beat inflation. There is a choice of investment terms (for how long you can invest). You may invest from £100 up to £15,000 in each issue tax-free.
■ *Fixed interest savings certificates* Guaranteed interest rates will give you peace of mind. There is a choice of investment terms. Again, you may invest from £100 to £15,000 in each issue tax-free.

The NS&I also offers premium bonds, which are a different kind of saving and are described separately at the end of this chapter.

NS&I guaranteed returns

In addition to the index-linked and fixed interest savings certificates, NS&I also offers three types of savings bonds with a choice of investment terms from one year to five years:

■ *Fixed rate savings bonds* You can opt for high growth/low income bonds or low growth/high income bonds. You may invest from £500 up to £1 million. Interest is paid net of tax. Choice of investment terms.
■ *Capital bonds* Fixed interest rates rise over five years with a guaranteed lump sum at the end of the term. You may invest from £100 up to £1 million. On these bonds, interest is paid gross of tax.
■ *Pensioners guaranteed income bonds* Exclusively available to those aged 60 and over, these bonds offer a guaranteed monthly income. The interest is paid gross of tax.

Other NS&I bonds

There is one other type of NS&I bond offering monthly income at competitive but variable rates:

▌ *Income bonds* Again, you can invest from £500 up to £1 million. Higher rates are offered on investments over £25,000.

Finally, high potential returns are almost assured from:

▌ *Guaranteed equity bonds* You can benefit from the growth potential offered by the FTSE 100 (the *Financial Times* index listing 100 top London Stock Exchange shares) over five years. The value of your original investment is guaranteed and you may invest from £100 to £30,000.

Bank and building society savings accounts and bonds

There is a vast array of savings accounts and income and capital bonds offered by the leading banks and building societies designed for adults rather than children. These products offer similar or rather better interest rates than the comparable NS&I products – with the difference that they are not backed by the government.

You can carry out the comparisons for yourself. As before, the rates, terms and conditions of leading providers are listed on the Financial Services Authority website (www.fsa.gov.uk) and in the national weekday and Sunday Press.

Life and term assurance

Life assurance is one of the ways in which we can provide for the security of our families in the event of our own or another member of the family's death. There are two basic forms of life assurance: investment-type life insurance and term insurance.

Investment-type life insurance

We've already come across investment-type life assurance as one of the categories of investment approved for ISAs. There are six specific types of this kind of life assurance:

■ whole-of-life insurance;
■ with-profits bonds;
■ unit-linked bonds;
■ income and growth bonds;
■ endowment policies;
■ maximum investment plans; and
■ other life insurance that build up a cash-in.

Investment-type life insurance pays up if you die, except for whole-of-life insurance, which also pays up if you don't. However, whole-of-life insurance costs much more than protection-only insurance and you should consider it in comparison with other investment products. Having regard to the appalling recent record of endowment assurance in relation to mortgages and pension funds, you will be wise to shun this type of insurance completely.

Term insurance

Term insurance is often the cheapest way to buy all the cover you need to protect your family. It pays out if you die within a set period of time (the 'term') but if you survive the term it pays out nothing. Therefore, the monthly or annual premiums are lost as soon as you survive the month or year to which they relate.

Term insurance also includes mortgage protection policies that you may take out to cover the period until your mortgage is repaid. If you have a repayment mortgage, you may be able to secure lower premiums by accepting reductions in cover in line with the reduced balance of your outstanding mortgage.

Term insurance is not an investment and, strictly speaking, it is not saving either. However, it is a way to spend your surplus cash to ensure that your survivors can maintain their standard of living.

Important points to take into account are:

■ Smokers pay much higher premiums than non-smokers (in some cases more than twice as much).
■ The premium may be higher if your health is poor, or you take part in risky activities.
■ The premium may be higher, or cover refused altogether, if your lifestyle puts you at added risk of contracting HIV/AIDS.

■   Check for exclusions. Most policies do not cover death due to alcohol or drug abuse. You might not be covered while taking part in risk sports.

■   Premiums are usually fixed for the whole term.

■   You get tax relief on premiums if you take out life cover through a personal pension or a stakeholder pension. However, the life insurance element will be taken as part of the maximum you can pay into your personal pension (see Chapter 7).

■   Check whether you can reduce or increase cover easily if your circumstances change and, if so, at what cost.

■   By paying an extra premium, you can usually include a 'waiver of premium' if you are unable to work because of a long-term illness.

There are some options on term life insurance policies. They can be written so that your family receives a single lump sum payment if you die. Alternatively, you can take out a:

■   *family benefit policy*, which pays income rather than a lump sum;

■   *increasing policy*, where cover and premium rise over the years;

■   *renewable policy*, which lets you extend the original term.

Death benefits are currently free of UK income tax and capital gains tax, but may be subject to inheritance tax.

Financial advice

When you approach an insurance company for a quotation on a term insurance policy, one of the first questions that you will be asked is whether you have an independent financial adviser. This is because there have been prosecutions, fines and many claims for damages following the dodgy selling practices of some insurance and pension providers or their agents. These cases have arisen mainly in the case of endowment assurance and personal pension and retirement plans. Not surprisingly, insurance companies are now nervous of claims and do everything possible to protect themselves within the law.

Even in the case of term insurance policies you will be cautioned that any representative of the company can only advise you on that insurance company's products and that only an independent adviser can advise you on the products available from other companies. As from 14 January 2005, all term insurance advisers have to be authorized by the FSA.

You will find more about financial advisers in general in Part 4. For now you may decide that dealing with some leading insurance companies is painful enough without further complications – particularly with those that you can approach only through call centres located thousands of miles away from the United Kingdom.

Premium bonds

Premium bonds are quite unlike any other form of saving, partly because they do not pay any interest and partly because you have the outside chance of receiving large sums of money from the monthly draws. However, they are a safe form of saving because they are a National Savings and Investments (NS&I) product, which means that they are fully backed by HM Treasury.

How premium bonds work

Monitored by NS&I, there is a draw every month, which delivers over 1 million tax-free prizes of varying amounts from £50 to £100,000 with a single jackpot of £1 million.   *50*

You can invest from a minimum of £100 up to £30,000 in premium bond certificates. However, NS&I can only accept applications from residents of the United Kingdom, Channel Islands and Isle of Man, due to gaming and lottery laws outside the United Kingdom.

You can cash in your bonds and recover your money any time you like. In addition, if you change your mind about buying premium bonds within 14 days of receiving your welcome letter, your money will be refunded or NS&I will help you to find another product within their portfolio which suits your needs better.

What kind of return can you expect?

There is absolutely no guarantee of success in the monthly draws. However, the notional return, based on many years' experience, is 3.2 per cent a year, although the return is irregular and you may receive nothing for many months. NS&I claim in their advertising that with average luck someone investing £30,000 could win 15 prizes a year. Surprisingly, many prizes are not claimed.

The bottom line is that your savings remain safe, although the capital value will be eroded by inflation. Unlike the National Lottery, where you lose your stake every time that you fail, your premium bonds are entered again and again into each monthly draw after registration and remain recoverable. You can also invest online by visiting www.nsandi or by calling (0500) 007 007.

Case history

A few years ago, the managing director of a medium-sized firm, having taken a beating like everyone else on the stock market, decided to buy £10,000 of premium bonds. Five years and nine months later, the original sum has grown, through regular prizes, to £11,550. The gain of £1,550 is tax-free, which is an important advantage to this 40 per cent taxpayer. The tax-free return works out at approximately 2.7 per cent – not dramatic, but the capital is absolutely safe. And there's always a tiny chance of that £1 million prize!

Checklist

1. If your child was born after 1 September 2002, the government will provide a payment voucher of £250 to open a Child Trust Fund (CTF) registered in your child's name.
2. Family and friends can add up to a further £1,200 per birthday year and money can be taken out when the child reaches 18, free from income and capital gains tax.
3. For other children, banks and building societies offer cash deposit accounts where the interest will be paid without tax being taken off. National Savings and Investment (NS&I) offers government guaranteed bonus bonds that can be purchased for any child under 16.
4. If you give money to your child outside the CTF scheme on which the income earned is more than £100 per year, it will be taxed as if it is yours. Young people cannot hold an ISA until they are 18, so you can avoid tax by using your ISA to save for them.

5. All NS&I products are government-backed and are detailed on its website (www.nationalsavings.co.uk). You can invest up to £93,000 tax-free in various NS&I bonds and savings including premium bonds, Cash Mini ISAs and index-linked and fixed interest savings certificates.

6. NS&I also offers guaranteed returns bonds, including one available only to those over 60 where the interest is paid gross of tax. It also offers competitive income and guaranteed equity bonds. You can check them out against the products of other providers on www.fsa.gov.uk

7. Life and term insurance provide for the security of your family in the event of your death. Investment-type life insurance involves financial investments of various kinds and is covered in Part 4. Term insurance only pays out if you die within a set period of time. Premium payments are lost as soon as you survive the period to which they relate.

8. Death benefits are currently free of UK income tax and capital gains tax.

9. Term insurance policies can take several forms including policies that pay out income rather than a lump sum, policies where cover and premiums rise over the years and policies that let you extend the original period of your insurance. Only an independent financial adviser authorized by the FSA can advise you on the competitive products of a range of companies.

10. Don't ignore premium bonds as a safe form of cash investment up to £30,000, which could produce a spectacular return if you are lucky.

7 Pensions

This one chapter makes no attempt to cover a big topic thoroughly. Indeed, whole books have been and will continue to be written on the subject of pensions for the benefit of consumers, employers and the self-employed. What I have tried to do in this third chapter under the heading of Passive Saving is to explain the various kinds of pension that are available to the individual today, the factors in taking a decision on the type of pension that suits you best and where to go for pensions advice.

Perhaps you should first consider what are the advantages and disadvantages of investing in pensions over and above the state pensions to which you are entitled anyway, as a result of national insurance contributions that you have made or which have been made on your behalf. The attraction of the occupational and personal pension schemes described below is that you are building up over your working life a capital sum that can be invested at retirement, usually in an annuity, to provide assured income for your remaining years. However, a pension is a long-term investment; you can't touch the money you put into your pension scheme until you reach retirement age.

Further advantages of personal and occupational schemes are that your contributions up to prescribed limits, discussed below, are eligible for tax relief and, in the case of personal pension schemes, you may set a retirement date, at present from age 50, when the pension will mature. (The state pension age is 65.) You can also take a tax-free lump sum on retirement up to 25 per cent of the total capital value of your pension fund.

Potential disadvantages of pension schemes include the consequences of not being able to keep up your pension contributions, in the case of unemployment or long-term illness. Some schemes make provision for you to take a contribution 'holiday', but the bottom line is that if you stop paying into your pension permanently the value of your fund will not increase further and you will not be able to recover any capital sum or income until the agreed retirement date when the scheme matures. If this happens in the early years of the scheme, when the set-up charges are debited against your contributions, the accrued value may well be less than the total of your contributions to date and you may still have to wait until the maturity date to get your cashback.

One disadvantage of all non-state pensions schemes, except for those occupational schemes of the 'final salary' type (see below), is that there is no certainty about the amount of income that you can swap your pension fund for at retirement. This is because the annuity rates (the income that you can buy with a lump sum) are determined not only by your age but by your life expectancy based on the statistical evidence at the time. With people continuing to live longer, it is likely that annuity rates will have declined further by the time you retire.

You may decide that there are other priorities over the long-term commitment of saving through a pension scheme, such as life assurance protection for you and your family or 'rainy day' cash saving of the kinds that we have described in the last chapter. Remember that you can always purchase an annuity with your cash savings when you reach retirement age and you will be able to gain tax relief on lump sum pension fund contributions from April 2006 under the new tax regime described later in the chapter.

Pensions are one area of saving where you certainly need good advice, so, before making up your mind you would do well to consult an independent financial adviser, authorized by the FSA and specializing in pensions. This is especially true at the present time because there are big changes coming when the present regimes for occupational and personal pension schemes are rationalized into a single regime, with effect from 5 April 2006, which has been christened 'A-day'. Since April 2005, the FSA has published on its website, www.fsa.gov.uk, revised versions of all its pensions literature, including details of the new tax regime, which gives you and your adviser time to plan ahead.

If you want to take advantage of the free advice offered by the Pensions Advisory Service, you can contact the OPAS Pensions Helpline on (0845) 601 2923 or visit its website at www.stakeholderhelpline.org.uk. Alternatively, if you decide to appoint an independent financial adviser you can obtain a shortlist of three such local advisers from which to make your selection by telephoning IFA Promotions on (0800) 085 3250.

Types of pension

Currently in 2005, there are four potential sources of pensions for your retirement income:

▌ *the basic state pension* for those who've paid national insurance contributions while at work or who have been credited with contributions;
▌ *the additional state pension*, now the state second pension, and also dependent on national insurance contributions;
▌ *an occupational pension* through an employer's pension scheme;
▌ *a personal pension scheme* (including stakeholder schemes) open to everyone and especially useful if you are self-employed or your employer does not run a company scheme.

State pensions

You are unlikely to receive enough income to live on from state pensions, certainly not in the style you've been used to when working, although under current regulations you would be able to claim means-tested state benefits if you have no other source of income. From 6 April 2005, the basic state pension was £82.05 a week for a single person and £49.15 for an adult dependent. There are also weekly pension allowances for dependent children of £9.55 for the eldest child and £11.35 for each other child.

Before 6 April 2002, you were able to build up SERPS (state earnings related pension scheme) as the state second pension. Today's state second pension is available to employees earning more than a given minimum (£79 a week from 6 April 2004). If you are caring for young children or, perhaps, an elderly relative or suffer from a disability or long-term illness, you are also able to build up a state second pension.

Plainly, one of your major concerns is how you can build up an additional retirement fund. The longer you leave it to start a pension fund, the older you get and the more expensive it becomes to build up a worthwhile fund. The rest of this chapter is devoted to describing contributory pension schemes that will help you to achieve that objective.

Occupational pensions

If you work for an employer who runs a pension scheme, it's probably a good idea to join. Traditionally, employers' pension schemes were contributory, which means that you make contributions by deduction of salary, or non-contributory, when the employee makes no contribution. In either case, your employer must contribute to the scheme on your behalf, although there may be periods of time when the employer does not contribute.

A typical package of the benefits that you get from joining a good employer's scheme would include the following:

■ A taxable pension from the company's normal retirement age (often 65 but sometimes lower – as for doctors until recently).
■ Annual increases to the pension once you start receiving it (some pension annuities have no built-in inflation provision).
■ A tax-free lump sum at retirement (currently limited to 25 per cent of the capital value of the pension).
■ The possibility of retiring earlier, but on a reduced pension (currently under review – you may be able in the future to start drawing your pension early without stopping work).
■ A pension if ill health causes you to retire early.
■ Pensions for your married partner and other dependents if you die first.
■ Life insurance that pays a lump sum to your dependents if you die first.

Employer pension schemes are funded to generate benefits according to one of two types. Either, 1. *final salary* (also called 'defined benefit'), where the promised pension is calculated according to a formula based on your pay and the length of time that you have been with the company in the scheme (if you leave the scheme before the retirement date the promised pension will probably be lower). Or, 2. *money purchase* (also called 'defined contribution'). The amount of pension you get depends on the amount paid in, how well your investment grows, the amount deducted in charges and the rate at which you can swap the amount of your pension fund for actual pension at retirement.

The final salary type of scheme is generally much more expensive for the company to fund and is more risky both for the employer, and for the employee too if the scheme is under-funded and the trustees cannot pay out the promised benefits. During the last 10 years, there have been some spectacular pension fund failures, which generally came to light when the company itself got into financial trouble. The problem was compounded by the ability of trustees to take contribution 'rests', that is, to stop paying into the pension fund, when the actuaries to the fund managers (we met them in the last chapter) advised that there were surplus funds to meet all retirement commitments. In the United Kingdom, a high proportion of pension fund money was invested in stocks and shares; so, when the stock market fell, surpluses turned suddenly into losses and many pension schemes remain under-funded to this day.

Even worse, trustees were empowered to use some of their pension funds to purchase shares in the company itself and, since trustees were sometimes the directors of a failing company, it is not surprising that many of these 'self-investments' proved fatal.

As a result of the pension fund failures, defined benefit schemes are offered less frequently. Many of the loopholes have been closed and there are some important changes to the law coming shortly that will affect employers further. Most companies are no longer willing to take the risk of pension scheme under-funding.

Some companies have even taken steps to convert their final salary schemes to defined contribution schemes. Therefore, if you join a company today you will probably be offered a money purchase scheme. A money purchase scheme is likely to provide a lower pension income than a final salary scheme, if everything goes according to plan, but at least the company's funding requirement is constant and certain. Trustees have less scope for mistakes or maladministration.

Advanced voluntary contributions (AVCs)

If you are a member of an occupational pension scheme you may be able to supplement the benefits you receive by topping up your contributions. Most occupational pension schemes offer you the opportunity to make additional voluntary contributions (AVCs), usually in the form of money purchase pensions where you build up a capital sum and cash it in on retirement for an annuity. The main features of AVC schemes are:

- Tax relief on contributions.
- Ability to stop or vary your contributions as you may wish.
- Usually low or nil charges (your employer may pay towards them).
- The total of your AVC contributions and your contributions to the occupational scheme cannot be more than 15 per cent of your salary (up to April 2006 when the rules change).

▌ Some final salary schemes provide 'added years' AVCs, which means that your years of service with the employer can be increased to give a bigger pension based on your final salary.

▌ Very occasionally, some final salary schemes make provision for your employer to match or subsidize contributions to the AVC scheme by paying extra amounts.

There are two disadvantages under the current pensions' regime: 1. You can't convert part of your pension into a tax-free lump sum, if you started your AVC scheme after April 1987, unless it's of the added years variety. 2. You can't take your AVC scheme with you if you change jobs. However, if you earn less than £30,000 per year you can contribute to a stakeholder pension scheme instead of (or as well as) an AVC.

Personal pensions

There are three types of personal pension:

▌ stakeholder pensions;
▌ occupational pensions (other than those offered by employers);
▌ group personal pension schemes.

You also need to be aware of self-invested personal pension schemes (SIPPs). A SIPP plan is a tax-efficient wrapper within which you can hold a wide range of investments.

Cost penalties

The starting point for all personal pensions is that they involve costs. Unlike an employer's occupational pension scheme where the employer's scheme pays all the costs of setting up the pension, you will have to pay the costs yourself. In the past, the setting up and management charges have taken a big bite out of your savings, particularly if you committed yourself to save regularly but then had to stop. Reasons for stopping might be that you have lost your job, have been given the opportunity to join an occupational scheme or stopped work to have a baby. The FSA notes that as many as one person in four who starts a personal plan stops paying within three years. In that event, you will see part, even all, of your savings eaten up by the costs of setting up the plan.

Since April 2001, the situation has improved. A personal pension will qualify as a stakeholder pension if the conditions include:

- low charges;
- flexible contributions;
- no extra charges if you transfer to another scheme.

It certainly makes sense to consider a stakeholder pension if you are starting a new personal pension. However, switching from an existing personal pension to a stakeholder scheme may not save you from the bulk of personal pension charges that you have already paid. If in doubt, consult an independent financial adviser – although that may cost you too.

Stakeholder pensions

The best way to brief yourself thoroughly on stakeholder pensions is to use the FSA fact sheet containing separate 'decision trees' for employed people (not in a company pension scheme), the self-employed and anyone who is not employed but who might be able to contribute to a personal pension. Basically, stakeholder pensions were designed for lower income families.

Decision trees

The decision trees are in two parts. The first part consists of introductory notes describing what a stakeholder pension is and how it works. The notes also give details of the state pension scheme and list some of the questions you might want to ask.

In the second part, you will find flowcharts that ask you questions about your present pension arrangements and personal circumstances. The answers to these questions will help you to consider your pension options. The stakeholder pension decision trees themselves give some pension estimates based on your age and how much you can afford to contribute regularly to a stakeholder pension.

The decision trees are available online in an interactive version where you enter your details and requirements and the calculation is made for you. Visit http://www.fsa.gov.uk and search for 'decision trees'. Available to download in PDF at http://www.fsa.gov.uk/pubs/other/badged_decision_trees.pdf.

Pension calculator

For help in working out how much pension your savings might produce there is also a pension calculator prepared jointly by the Association of British Insurers (ABI) and the FSA, which is another interactive service available to you on the website www.pensioncalculator.org.uk, linked to the consumer section of the general FSA website.

There is no guarantee attached to the pension calculator estimates. Nevertheless, it is a useful crystal ball based on the following assumptions:

▌ *Investment growth* Your pension fund will grow by 7 per cent a year until you retire.

▌ *Inflation* The Retail Prices Index (RPI) will rise by 2.5 per cent a year until you retire.

▌ *Pension fund charges* The company providing your pension will charge 1 per cent of your fund each year.

▌ *Income tax rebates* The government will add a tax rebate to your contributions at the basic rate (22 per cent), so that every £1 that goes into your fund consists of 78p from you and 22p from the government.

▌ *Annuity rates* When you retire your pension fund is used to buy a pension income, called an annuity. Estimated annuity rates are used in the calculator based on your retirement age.

▌ *Average life expectancy.*

The pension calculator estimates also assume that you keep up regular monthly payments until you retire and increase your monthly payments each year by a minimum of the estimated rate of inflation (2.5 per cent).

In 20 years' time, at the estimated 2.5 per cent rate of inflation, £1,000 will buy only the same as £600 today. Therefore, the pension calculator works out what the real buying power of your estimated pension income will be when you retire, known as 'today's prices'.

In Table 7.1 I have set out some examples of pension calculator estimates based on the above assumptions, which will give you a rough idea of what you can expect.

I have also included for each example the calculation of what your weekly pension might be if you save 10 per cent more each month or retire five years later. Monthly contributions have been held at £100 throughout for comparison purposes.

Table 7.1 Examples of pension calculator estimates

Age 5/4/04	Male/ female	Gross earnings per year £	Monthly payment £	Retirement age	Lump sum £	Weekly income at today's prices £
25	M	15,000	100	65	no	133
			110	65	no	140
			100	70	no	201
25	F	15,000	100	60	25,000	62
			110	60	25,000	68
			100	65	25,000	90
25	M	15,000	100	65	31,000	99
			110	65	31,000	109
			100	70	31,000	150
25	F	15,000	100	60	no	82
			110	60	no	90
			100	65	no	120
35	M	30,000	100	65	no	71*
			110	65	no	79*
			100	70	no	108*
35	F	25,000	100	60	no	49
			110	60	no	53
			100	65	no	74
45	M	45,000	100	65	10,000	30*
			110	65	10,000	34*
			100	70	10,000	48*
45	F	35,000	100	60	no	25
			110	60	no	27
			100	65	no	42

Notes:
1   Basic contributions have been held throughout at £100 per month.
2   * Identifies pensions that provide a half-pension for spouse or partner

Source: ABI and FSA Pension Calculator 2 January 2005

Contracting out of the state second pension

You can use a stakeholder pension scheme to contract out of the state second pension, but it requires careful consideration. Everyone in employment above the lower earnings limit set by the government is automatically included in the state second pension unless they are contracted out through an employer's occupational pension scheme, or they decide to leave it.

If you 'contract out' you give up your state second pension entitlement and instead build up a replacement for it in your own private pension arrangement, typically a stakeholder pension. Deciding to contract out in one tax year does not commit you to do the same in later years, but you should really take advice on what is the best thing for you to do.

Occupational pensions (group personal pension schemes)

If an employer has five or more employees it is normally required by law to give its staff access to a stakeholder pension. The Occupational Pensions Regulatory Authority (OPRA) will help you to investigate whether your employer should do so, if it has not given you access to a stakeholder pension already.

Some employers offer pension arrangements called 'group personal pension schemes'. They are effectively personal pensions and are therefore covered by the rules and conditions for personal pension plans outlined above. However, a group personal pension scheme can have advantages over taking out a personal pension plan by yourself if your employer pays into the plan on your behalf (these contributions will stop if you change your job); has negotiated special terms with the provider, such as reduced costs or flexible contributions.

Self-invested personal pension schemes (SIPPs)

A SIPP operates in the same way as a conventional personal pension in respect of contributions and eligibility for Inland Revenue purposes, except that you and/or your advisers have control over the investment choice.

A SIPP must be set up with a recognized provider and professional trustee. The range of permitted investments is wide and includes the more conventional financial investments (which you will read about in Part 4) such as:

■ deposits;
■ unit trusts;
■ stocks and shares;
■ less usual assets such as commercial property or loans.

Protection
SIPPs are not protected by the Financial Services Compensation Scheme (FRCS) because the SIPP wrapper itself is not regulated by the FSA.

Depending on what they are, some investments through a SIPP can be protected. For example, if the provider of an investment held in a SIPP fails and is unable to repay funds you have invested, or an adviser who has advised you badly is unable to pay redress, the FRCS may provide protection. However, not all claimants are eligible to make a claim for compensation from the FRCS.

If you want to set up a SIPP after you have read Part 4, to be safe, you really should consult an independent financial adviser. The best timing for starting a SIPP will be shortly after April 2006 when the range of permitted investments is extended. For example, if you own your own business through a limited company, the shares will be an eligible investment for your SIPP.

You can start making the arrangements well in advance of April 2006. If all this seems too much trouble in relation to the depth of your pocket, you're probably better to stick to a stakeholder pension.

Tax relief

Under present tax arrangements the Inland Revenue will pay an extra 28p for each £1 that you pay into your stakeholder pension fund, even if you don't normally pay income tax. However, there are limits set by the Inland Revenue on how much you can contribute to a stakeholder pension, which depend on your taxable earnings and age. There are also special limits for people who are members of employers' occupational pension schemes and for those without any earnings.

Currently, most people can contribute up to £3,600 in any tax year to a stakeholder pension, including basic-rate tax relief. Therefore, if you pay in £2,808 the income tax relief would raise your contribution to the £3,600 limit. Even if you have no paid employment, you can still set up a stakeholder pension and then benefit from tax relief on your contributions, although you don't pay a penny in income tax.

If you are in non-pensionable employment or self-employed, you may be able to contribute more than £3,600 and still get income tax relief, depending on your age and earnings. At present, you can contribute 17.5 per cent of your earnings in any tax year and gain relief up to the age of 35. If you are older there is a scale that allows you to contribute higher percentages of your income allowable before tax as you continue to grow older. If you pay income tax at the higher rate (40 per cent) you will be able to claim back the extra tax at the end of the tax year. However, this regime will change drastically on A-day (5 April 2006), as the next section explains.

After A-day – the new pensions regime

The main changes to pensions, other than the extended range of investments eligible for SIPPs, that the government proposes and that may affect your financial planning are:

∎ From April 2005, you are able to put off starting to receive your state pension indefinitely and earn an increase in the pension when it does start for each year that it has been deferred. Alternatively, you will be able to convert the increase into a cash sum.

∎ While the state pension age remains at 65, the earliest age from which an occupational or personal pension may be taken will increase from 50 to 55 by 2010.

∎ You will be able to draw an occupational pension from your employer's scheme while continuing to work for that employer.

∎ From April 2006, the current limits on annual contributions and retirement benefit amounts will be replaced by a single lifetime limit on the amount of pensions savings built up that qualify for the advantageous tax relief.

∎ The lifetime limit will start at £1.5 million in 2006 and will increase each year up to £1.8 million in 2010. Any assets in your pension fund that exceed the lifetime allowance at retirement will be taxed at 55 per cent.

∎ If you already have a pension fund and you estimate that the asset value will exceed £1.5 million at April 2006, you can register your funds on A-day or up to three years after, to protect them from the charge.

∎ From A-day, there will be two types of protection:
  – Primary protection preserves any excess you may have in an existing pension fund above the £1.5 million limit. As the cap rises, so does your tax-free entitlement by the amount of your excess at April 2006.
  – Enhanced protection is available if your fund will be below the £1.5 million cap at April 2006 but you expect that it will climb over the limit before your retirement date. Registration will protect

your fund from any future increase above the cap, but you must stop all pension contributions before A-day.

I There will be an annual limit on how much your pension fund can increase in value – in term of contributions and the value of benefits – starting at £215,000 in 2006, which will be increased each year in line with inflation.

I The tax-free lump sum you can take at retirement will continue to be 25 per cent after April 2006.

The effect of all these rather confusing changes is that you will be able to put much more into your pension and increase your annuity alternatives.

Pension-linked term assurance

Life cover that pays off if you die in the period up to retirement is a form of term insurance reviewed in Chapter 6. Since April 2001 it can be taken out through a personal pension scheme as a part of your stakeholder pension. Pension-linked term insurance is especially cheap, because you get tax relief on the premiums. However, the premiums do count with your actual pension contributions towards the maximum amount that is eligible for tax relief.

Investment-type life insurance can take the form of any of the following:

I whole-of-life insurance;
I with-profits bonds;
I unit-linked bonds;
I income and growth bonds endowment policies;
I endowment policies;
I maximum investment plans;
I other life insurance that builds up a cash-in value.

All of these effectively non-insurance products are defined in Part 4, Chapter 8.

We've already noted that whole-of-life insurance is much more expensive than term insurance and it is unsuitable as a pension-linked policy. It can provide a high level of cover for five or 10 years ahead, but after that expect the cost to rise or cover to be reduced.

Checklist

1. You are unlikely to receive enough income from state pensions to live on in the same way as you were before retirement. The state second pension is available to those in employment earning more than £79 per week.
2. An employer's occupational pension scheme usually involves compulsory contributions from the employer and contributions from employees who join. You can supplement your occupational pension by contributing to an advanced voluntary contribution scheme (AVC).
3. Employer pension schemes are either of the defined benefit (final salary) or defined contribution (money purchase) type. Defined benefit schemes are increasingly rare for new employees as a result of pension fund failures and under-funding in recent years. If you join a company today you will probably be offered a money purchase scheme.
4. Starting up a personal pension scheme involves costs that you will have to pay yourself. If you stop paying into it within three years, part or all of your savings may have been eaten up. Study the new tax regimes, which come into effect on 'A-day', April 2006, and will alter the limit on tax allowable pension contributions and benefits.
5. Stakeholder pension schemes are less costly by regulation. But switching from an existing personal pension to a stakeholder scheme may not save you from most of the personal pension charges that you have already paid. You can also contract out of the state second pension and replace it with a stakeholder pension.
6. Brief yourself on stakeholder pensions by using the FSA fact sheet and decision trees to be found on http://www.fsa.gov.uk/pubs/other/badged_decision_trees.pdf.
7. Work out how much your savings might produce by consulting the pension calculator on website www.pensioncalculator.org.uk. Table 7.1 shows examples of some pension calculator estimates at today's prices and how much more your weekly pension might be if you pay more or retire later.

8. Group personal pension schemes offered through your employer can have advantages if your employer pays into the plan on your behalf or has negotiated special terms with the provider.
9. Self-invested pension schemes (SIPPs) are a 'wrapper' in which you can hold a wide range of investments controlled by yourself and/or your advisers. They qualify for the same tax relief on contributions as conventional personal pensions. A SIPP must be set up with a recognized provider and professional trustee.
10. Pension-linked term insurance is especially cheap because you receive tax relief on the premiums. But they do count towards the maximum relief allowed for pension contributions.

Part Four
Financial investment

8 Bonds and fixed interest securities

There is another distinction between savings and investment that the Financial Services Authority (FSA) offers: savings are money you might need to get at quickly or money you put aside for a purchase or expense that you know will come up fairly soon; investments are really for the longer term – money you can afford to put aside for five years or more. The FSA also cautions that investments are not guaranteed to return your money in full, particularly if you decide to cash-in within five years or a longer period.

In this chapter we review the different types of investment that are available and those that are most suitable for the individual investor like you and me. We start with bonds and fixed interest securities, which are generally at the safer end of the market. In Chapter 9, we move on to equities, which tend to be more speculative.

Basically, a bond is a tradable written obligation on the part of its issuer to fulfil a variety of conditions. The obligations usually relate to the payment of dividends and the repayment of capital. Some bonds have additional features, such as the option to convert into something else, such as company shares.

Key points about bonds

▌ Bonds can be converted into cash by selling them (the meaning of 'tradable').

▌ Bonds come with a definite 'use by' date attached at which they will repay their capital in full (the face value of the bond).

▌ Bonds can take the form of documents or they may exist as account entries with a custodian. Bearer bonds exist only as bits of paper.

▌ Bonds are used to raise money for the issuer, which may be a government, an institution or a company. They promise to pay you back your money after a fixed number of years. In the meantime, they pay you some money each year.

▌ Since the interest paid to a bond holder is usually fixed, bonds are also called 'fixed interest investments'.

▌ You can buy a bond when it is issued through your bank or stockbroker, or even direct from the issuer. Alternatively, you can buy it in the marketplace from someone else.

▌ Usually, you won't pay the face (nominal) value for a bond. It has a value or price that is agreed between the buyer and the seller through the medium of a recognized exchange or market. The price goes up and down constantly and is affected by the considerations explained below.

▌ Bonds are evaluated in terms of their 'yield', which is a measure of the financial return it will provide to the bond holder.

How the price mechanism works

Factors affecting the day-to-day prices of bonds are:

▌ current and expected market interest rates;
▌ current and expected inflation rate;
▌ the economic news of the day;
▌ the position of other bond markets around the world;
▌ the potential for further bond issues in the future.

All of these factors add up to what financial commentators and journalists call 'market sentiment'.

You can calculate a bond yield in many different ways. Most of them are basically the result of expressing payments received by a bond holder as a percentage of the purchase price. There are only two that you need to know about if you are considering an investment in bonds: 1. *running or flat yield*, which is the annual dividend divided by the purchase price and 2. *gross redemption yield*, which also takes into account the capital gain or loss to redemption (when the capital is paid back) in a more complex calculation. Yields are generally expressed as percentages. As the price of a bond rises, its yield will fall; and, as a bond price falls, the yield will rise.

Example 8.1

1. A £100 bond is issued with a face value of £100 paying interest at 5 per cent. The running yield on issue is 5 divided by 100 × 100 per cent = 5 per cent.
2. You buy the bond on the London Stock Exchange at a price of £90. The running yield for you is 5 divided by 90 × 100 per cent = 5.55 per cent.
3. You sell the bond at a price of £110. The running yield for the purchaser is 5 divided by 110 × 100 per cent = 4.55 per cent. (Incidentally, you made a profit of £20.)

Bond risks

If you hold a bond until the issuer repays the capital, known as 'holding to maturity', you know exactly what the outcome will be. You can work out precisely all future interest and capital repayment that you will receive and, therefore your financial return. In this sense, bonds and other fixed interest securities are viewed as low risk.

On the other hand, there are risks if you do not hold a bond to maturity. Fluctuating market prices may mean that you get less money back than you invested. In the example above, if you had bought at £110 and sold at £90 you would have lost, instead of gaining, £20.

There is also the risk that the issuer of a bond may default on its payment. This is generally higher than the risk of losing any money you may have in a bank cash account, but you do have some protection. Bond holders have a first call on any remaining assets in the case of company liquidation, after creditors, including the Inland Revenue and the workforce and certainly before the shareholders. The rights of a bond holder are detailed in the legal document that is attached to the bond.

UK government bonds have the highest credit ratings in the market. The government issues new debt to fund the difference between its expenditure and its receipts and to fund the servicing cost of the existing debt. The government always has the option of increasing taxation to raising new debt as a means to cover its budget deficit. British government bonds are often referred to as 'gilt-edged securities' or 'gilts' for short, because the chances of it being unable to pay the interest or refund the capital on its bonds as they mature are considered to be remote. In more than 100 years of history, the government has never failed to make a payment of interest or capital on its bonds as it falls due. By contrast, a corporate bond's credit rating is linked to the financial strength and prospects of the issuer. Ultimately, it is financed out of the profits of the company that issues them.

There are several independent credit agencies that rate the credit risk of bond issuers. The more risky will have to offer extra attractions in order to sell their bonds such as a higher yield, either a more attractive interest rate or by issuing the bond at a lower price than the redemption price, or both. Obviously, this is a more risky proposition than a government bond. Therefore, corporate bonds usually have a lower credit rating and a higher yield than gilts.

Who buys and sells bonds?

In most bond markets there are a variety of investors; the most important are:

- ▌ large investment banks who often deal in very large amounts over very short periods of time;
- ▌ institutional investors such as pension funds and insurance companies;
- ▌ fund management houses dealing on behalf of many individual private investors collectively.

Individual private investors are relatively insignificant in the market. There is no reason why they cannot buy bonds directly, particularly if intending to hold them to maturity. If you intend to take a shorter-term view, you are better to leave it to professional managers or, at least, take the advice of an independent financial adviser.

Leading types of bonds

This section describes the main types of bonds that a UK investor like yourself will probably come across.

Conventional UK government bonds

HM Treasury, through its Debt Management Office as agent, dominates the sterling bond market, that is, those bonds that are issued in £ sterling. The UK government gilt market is the benchmark against which all other sterling bonds are priced and rated.

Gilts usually trade off a lower yield than the bonds of other issuers. The lower return is the price you have to pay for the additional security. However, for a cautious investor, gilts are a prudent first choice.

There are around 35 actively traded conventional gilts at the moment, which together account for almost 75 per cent in value (some £250 billion) of all gilts issued by the government. They make fixed interest payments every six months and a capital repayment upon maturity.

Conventional gilts have names such as Treasury 4 per cent 2009, where the 4 per cent denotes the annual interest paid on each £100 nominal of the stock and 2009 is the year in which the gilt will be redeemed. Gilts are listed on the London Stock Exchange and the prices are published daily. If you want to see what they are and how they are priced, buy a copy of the *Financial Times* and look in the columns of the Companies and Markets section.

The government issues gilts throughout the year with different years to final maturity, typically 5, 10 and 30 years ahead. Gilts in issue will mature in nearly every year for the next 30 years. The longest maturity conventional gilt at the moment is dated for redemption in the year 2038.

Some conventional gilts were issued several years ago with double redemption dates, for example, Exchequer 12 per cent 2013/17. In such cases the government can redeem the gilt at any time between the two dates, provided that it has given appropriate notice. If prevailing interest rates are below the coupon rate, it will normally redeem as soon as possible, because it can refinance more cheaply by another gilt with a lower coupon.

Index-linked gilts

Nearly all the remaining 25 per cent by value of the gilt market is accounted for by index-linked gilts. Unlike conventional gilts, both the dividend payments (interest) and capital payments of index-linked gilts are linked to inflation.

The calculation is based on movements in the Retail Price Index (although this may be replaced in the future by the newer Consumer Price Index, which we met earlier in the discussion on inflation). The impact of inflation is accrued from the date that an index-linked gilt is issued to the value of both dividends and capital with an eight-month time lag, so that investors know what the value of the next dividend will be at all times. For example, if the level of prices has increased by 50 per cent over the life of an index-linked gilt, every £100 nominal will be redeemed at £150 and the original 2 per cent coupon interest rate will have become 3 per cent. In effect, you are almost guaranteed a real return from holding index-linked gilts to maturity and any interest, if it was lower than the inflation rate at any time, will be adjusted to cover the difference.

With this benefit, you might think that you should always choose an index-linked gilt over a conventional gilt, but that is not necessarily so because:

▌ They are 'less liquid' – harder to sell in the market than conventional gilts, which may lead to additional costs.
▌ If retail prices should start to fall and inflation becomes negative (deflation), the income from holding index-linked gilts will also fall.
▌ The government takes into account the special attractions of index-linked gilts and sells them at a higher price in the first place, offering a lower yield.

Index-linked gilts were first issued in 1981 when the government needed to raise large amounts of money from selling bonds. Institutional investors can use them as a hedge against inflation instead of the more volatile equities, which you will meet in the next chapter.

Undated gilts

There are also a small number of undated gilts with no specific redemption date. Together, they account for only about 1 per cent of the overall gilt market. The most widely known is probably 3.5 per cent War Loan. This type of gilt is the oldest of all and some of them date back to the 17th century when the Bank of England was established. Some of them have unusual features such as paying a dividend four times a year rather than twice.

Although they are undated, this doesn't mean that these gilts cannot be redeemed. Like a double-dated conventional gilt, the government may redeem them and is sure to do so if it can do so at a lower cost. However, they were first issued at a time when interest rates were generally lower than they are today and carry low coupons (maximum 4 per cent). Interest rates in the gilt market will have to fall below these levels before redemption by the government becomes likely.

The separation of dividends from capital payments

Up to 1997 you could only buy a gilt in its entirety – with the holder having the right to both dividends and the capital repayment on maturity. However, following a successful innovation in the United States, you can now buy and trade these two rights separately.

Such instruments are known as 'Strips' (Separately Traded and Registered Interest and Principal Securities). Only some gilts can be stripped. The return on holding such instruments comes through the capital gain achieved, which may have certain tax or financial planning advantages for high income earners.

Supranational bonds

The World Bank or the European Investment Bank and other 'supranational' bodies, which sit above individual nations in some respects, use bonds as a means of raising money for specific development projects. Although such bodies do not themselves have any powers to raise taxes, their debts are usually guaranteed by governments that do have such powers. The credit rating of supranational bonds is therefore usually very high and they trade at similar yields to UK government bonds. Often they pay interest just once a year instead of twice.

Corporate bonds

Corporate bonds are bonds issued by companies. The way in which they work is basically the same as for government and supranational bonds but there is a higher risk of default because the continuing ability of the company to make interest payments, and eventually repay the debt, is less certain.

A company cannot raise taxes, like a government, as a means of servicing or repaying its debts and its ability to raise prices as a way of generating more cash is limited by competition in its marketplace and the business environment generally. If sales drop and profits fall away, the company may lose the ability to pay off its long-term debts or to raise fresh finance for that purpose. For these reasons, corporate bonds tend to have higher yields than government bonds anyway. The riskier the company is considered to be by investment professionals when its bond is issued, the higher the yield will be.

Some bonds of large multinational companies that are rated by leading international credit agencies such as Standard & Poor's and Moody's are considered to be almost as safe a credit risk as government bonds. Their bonds will be priced to yield only a little more.

By international standards, the UK corporate bond market is relatively small but is growing rapidly. Pension funds in company accounts are now valued against corporate bond yields under new accountancy standards, which has increased the demand for corporate bonds. As a result, there has been an increased issuance of corporate bonds recently, particularly of long-dated bonds that match pension fund liabilities more closely.

High yield or junk bonds

The lowest investment rating grade from Standard & Poor's is BBB (AAA is the highest) and from Moody's is Baa (against Aaa as its highest). If a bond is rated below these lower levels it is termed a 'high yield' or 'junk' bond. Certain types of investor are not allowed to buy junk bonds as the possibility of default is considered too high.

As you would expect, junk bonds yield much more than other bonds. If they do not default they will provide a high return for an investor. Individual junk bonds are really not for the small private investor. However, if you like the idea of junk bonds you can spread the risk by buying high yield bond unit trusts or open-ended investment companies (OEICs) where a professional fund manager makes all the decisions for the private investor.

Convertible bonds

By definition, convertible bonds are bonds that can be converted, usually by the bond holder and according to predefined rules, into something else. Most often the 'something else' will be a specific number of shares in the same company that has issued the bond.

Since conversion is at a predetermined price, the convertible bond becomes more valuable if the price of the underlying company shares rises. On the other hand, the bond-like qualities of the convertible limit the downside risk. Reflecting these advantages, convertible bonds tend to have lower yields than the non-convertible variety.

Overseas bonds

You are not restricted to buying only those bonds that are denominated in sterling. There are similar government and corporate bond markets in nearly every country worldwide, with bonds available in almost every country.

Internationally, the bond markets of the United States, Japan and the eurozone are the largest. UK issuers, including the government, also issue bonds in foreign currencies. Any bond that is denominated in a currency other than that of the country in which it is issued and traded is generally known as a 'eurobond' – nothing to do with the euro currency. Each currency has its own level of official interest rates, usually set by its own central bank.

If you think that overseas bonds appear to offer higher yields or more attractive features than UK bonds, remember that the foreign exchange market is a key consideration and any sudden or sustained movement in exchange rates against sterling could completely wipe out any advantage and destroy the return on your investment.

As with junk bonds, investment in overseas bonds is best left to professional fund managers and you will find that there are plenty of overseas bond funds available to the UK private investor.

Checklist

1. A bond is an obligation on the part of the issuer to pay interest by way of dividends and to repay the capital in the future. Some bonds have additional features, such as an option to convert into company shares.
2. Bonds are used to raise money for the issuer, which may be a government, an institution or a company.
3. Since the interest paid to a bond holder is usually fixed, bonds are also called 'fixed interest investments'. The financial return to the bond holder is called its 'yield'. The running or flat yield is the annual dividend divided by the purchase price expressed in percentages.
4. If you hold a bond until the issuer repays the capital, called 'holding to maturity', you know exactly what your financial

return will be. If you don't hold a bond to maturity, you might get less money back than you invested.

5. UK government bonds, known as 'gilts', have among the highest credit ratings. The government has never failed to make a due payment of interest or capital.

6. Most gilts are priced to give lower yields than the bonds of other issuers as a reflection of their low risk. They usually pay dividend interest every six months and capital at maturity, typically 5, 10 or 30 years ahead.

7. Index-linked gilts offer dividend interest and capital payments adjusted to the retail price index. They almost guarantee you a real return if held to maturity but the government tends to sell them at a higher price offering a lower yield than conventional gilts.

8. The World Bank, the European Investment Bank and other supra-national bodies also offer guaranteed bonds in various currencies. Any bond that is denominated in a currency other than that of the country in which it is issued is known as a 'eurobond'.

9. Corporate bonds, similar to government bonds, are issued by companies. They have a higher risk rating and therefore offer higher yields. Some bonds of multinational companies with a low risk rating are priced to yield only a little more. Bonds rated below investment rating grades are higher yield bonds, also known as 'junk bonds'.

10. Convertible bonds can be converted into something else, usually company shares, according to predetermined rules. They become more valuable when the price of the underlying shares rises, but the downside risk is limited.

Much of the content of this chapter and some of the next two chapters, 9 and 10, is drawn from the text written by John Dawe, Research Manager, at Lloyds TSB Private Equity in Part 2 of *Handbook of Personal Wealth Management*, published by Kogan Page, 2005 ISBN 0 7494 4383 9.

9 Equities and derivatives

Definition of equities

Shares represent the risk-bearing part of a company's capital. Much of a company's debt is secured on its assets and has priority in the event of liquidation after the payment of preferred creditors, chiefly the workforce and the Inland Revenue. By contrast, shareholders are at the end of the queue for payment if a company becomes insolvent and its assets are distributed on liquidation.

On the other hand, a company is owned by its shareholders and a share in the company entitles its holder to participate in the profits, as well as any losses, that the company may produce. There are a variety of different types or classes of shares, but the two most common are ordinary shares, known as 'equities' or 'stock' (as in common stock) and preference shares.

Preference shares

We will deal with preferred shares first, which are of lesser interest. Conventional preference shares carry a fixed rate of interest, which is paid as dividends either once or twice a year. They are 'preferred' because the company is required to make the interest payments out of its profits after taxation, before declaring any dividend to ordinary shareholders.

Some preference shares are listed on the same stock exchange that lists the ordinary shares in a company. Their market prices may go up or down, according to the general level of interest rates or in relation to the company's credit rating. Some preference shares are described as 'cumulative' because they provide that, in the event of one or more missed interest payments, the value of the unpaid interest is accumulated to the capital value and interest is then payable on that increased amount.

Preference shares may be 'redeemable' or 'convertible'. Redeemable preference shares are those where the company has the right to buy back the shares at predetermined dates, either at the issue price or at a premium. Convertible preference shares are those that provide for conversion into ordinary shares at predetermined intervals and prices, at the option of the preference shareholder. In this respect, they are similar to convertible bonds, but less secure.

Preference shares are used less often than in the past as a means of raising capital, partly because the fixed interest cannot be charged to income before tax by the company and, for larger companies, because the corporate bond market now provides a more convenient way of raising funds without adding to the share capital.

For the private investor, preference shares are less risky than ordinary shares, but they are sometimes less marketable and do not offer comparable opportunities for capital gains.

Ordinary shares

Ordinary shares usually come with voting rights attached, with each share having an equal voting right. In theory, individual shareholders together can exercise some control over the company, in particular the appointment of directors at shareholders' meetings. In practice, unless a shareholder owns a large proportion of the shares in issue or can band together with other sizeable shareholders, any idea of control is an illusion. All ordinary shares are issued with a nominal value, for example, £1 per share or 10p per share.

Most tradable shares are listed on a recognized investment exchange, such as the London Stock Exchange. As in the case of bonds, their actual value is set in the marketplace and share price information is published widely in the media and on the internet. Investor rewards come from holding the shares until the price appreciates, and also by way of any dividends that the company pays out during the waiting period.

What makes equities tick

The chance of making an exceptional gain over a relatively short period is one of the attractions of equities. That is why investors compete to purchase the new shares issued by a company on the London Stock Exchange. If applications exceed the number of shares available, there is an 'over-subscription', sometimes by many times, and the share price goes up. Investors who apply for many shares, perhaps more than they can afford, with the intention of selling them off quickly at a profit are called 'stags'. Of course, if more shares are then offered for sale than there is demand for, the price will come down again. You don't want to get caught in the rush.

Stagging is by no means a sure-fire way of making money and the costs of selling may well exceed any tiny profit per share made. However, stagging can be a very profitable activity for the wary.

The rewards of equity investment over longer periods can be spectacular. An original investment of $1,000 in Microsoft, the global software giant, at the beginning of the 1980s would have risen in value to more than $500,000 at the end of the 1990s. Employees who exercised their options to buy shares and took their gains became instant millionaires.

Equally, there are as many stories of failure as there are of success. Remember that when a quoted company in which you have invested fails completely, you are left with worthless shares. A recent UK example is that of Marconi, the long-established telecommunications technology company, whose share price crashed from 1250p to 50p in one year and to less than 1p two years later. There is no protection against hostile business conditions or poor management. Equities are definitely a risky form of investment in comparison to cash, bonds, or property, given that the value of a factory, office or house will hardly fall to zero.

The chance of an exceptional gain with little regard for possible loss – the greed factor – is one driving force for investment in equities but does not explain why the greater part of private investors' holdings have been in equities over many years. A part of the answer is that over time equities have beaten all other forms of investment for performance. The underlying reasons for superior performance are:

▌ The purpose of trading as a company is to achieve a return from the capital employed that is greater than the return available from simply putting the same capital on cash deposit or investing it in gilts. If a company can't do that, it should not be in business.

▌ A company has a degree of control over its own destiny. It is able to raise prices, cut costs, expand or contract production, introduce new products and interact generally with its suppliers, customers and competitors. By these actions companies can grow with the economy and outpace inflation. As a company grows, so should its profits and share price.

On the downside, the risk is that the directors of a company may choose a mistaken strategy or that management fails to carry out the company's strategy. This is where professional investment management, rather than the individual investor, is more likely to succeed by:

▌ focusing upon established companies that have a track record of success;
▌ analysing the accounts of companies in selected growth industries to eliminate those at risk of failure;
▌ spreading the risks by investing in a range of companies over selected industries, known as 'portfolio investment'.

All of these factors play out over a period of time. The longer that you hold a portfolio of equities, the more likely it is to perform well, if only because volatility will be less as market ups and downs will be smoothed out. If you hold equities for only a few years, short-term ups and downs may blot out any gain and leave you with a loss if you should need to sell. Over longer periods, such as 20 years or more, the short-term movements are likely to be lost within a more significant trend, which, on past history, is likely to be upwards.

Since 1945, there has been no 20-year period when UK equities have lost value. Their average return on capital only has been more than 500 per cent, ignoring dividend income and the effects of both inflation and taxation. Although this sounds impressive, it is equivalent to a quite modest 10 per cent each year over 20 years. Allowing for inflation and the reinvestment of dividend income, UK equities have produced an average return of some 350 per cent over 20-year periods since 1945, equivalent to 8 per cent a year. That compares favourably to UK government bonds, which produced little more than an average 2 per cent a year.

We should also take dividend income into account. Dividends paid by companies are at the discretion of the company (effectively, the shareholders in the General Meeting approving the directors' recommendation). Successful companies usually increase their dividends each year to reflect their earnings and profits growth, which can therefore keep up with or even outpace inflation. Very successful companies can distribute much bigger dividend payments over shorter periods of time. Examples are Tesco, which raised its dividends by more than 50 per cent between 2000 and 2004, and Lloyds TSB, the high street bank whose dividend increased by more than 150 per cent from 1996 to 2001.

So far, all these factors and the interplay between them, seems very logical. However, there are wild cards that can distort the share prices of individual shares or, indeed, whole sectors of the market. We have already identified the greed factor that causes investors to invest emotively in what appear to be exceptionally profitable opportunities or in shares that are tipped heavily by financial journalists and others. Sometimes, these tips may relate to start-up companies – such as those that attracted over the top ratings during the dot.com bubble of 1999/2000. Other tips may be for the shares of companies that are considered likely to become targets for takeover, although not necessarily doing well themselves.

At this point, you may ask yourself why, if share tipsters are so clever, they don't follow their own advice and become millionaires. The only case I can think of is Jim Slater, whose advice we refer to in the next chapter. George Soros, the billionaire who famously sold the £ sterling forward in 1995 just before sterling crashed, certainly followed his own advice but he wasn't a financial tipster. He was a currency trader who bet heavily on his own forecast and won.

Where this kind of investment sentiment becomes widespread across the stock market, it is said to be a 'bull' market. More bulls rush in as prices rise, anxious not to miss out on potential profits, and this pushes share prices even higher.

The flip side of greed is the fear factor: fear of missing out and fear of losing your money. When markets fall fast, investors may rush to sell in order to take whatever profits are left or to minimize losses. This process drives share prices down further. Markets falling in this way are described as 'bear' markets. Plunging share prices across the market as a whole, or particular sectors, can be a correction for previous overvaluation.

Another way of looking at it is that in bull or bear markets, investors are simply following their herd instinct. A stampede of raging bulls in the end may cause an upward market to collapse. Fortunately, most downward trends are halted before a retreat of bears becomes a rout.

Overseas equities

There are many thousands of companies quoted on overseas stock exchanges. You can invest in some industries globally on the London Stock Exchange through British companies that are global players in their sectors. Examples are BP in oils and GlaxoSmithKline in pharmaceuticals. There are other sectors such as automobiles, retailing or real estate where

UK companies have little overseas exposure and you can only invest in those industries globally through overseas company shares.

As we suggest more generally in the next chapter, it is sensible to invest in overseas companies through collective funds such as unit trusts or open-ended investment companies (OEICs), perhaps with a regional or industry focus, where the fund managers have specialist knowledge and experience of overseas investment. Prominent overseas stock markets include those of New York, Tokyo, Hong Kong and Singapore, as well as the stock exchanges of the United Kingdom's eurozone partners in the EU.

Don't forget that the same words of caution regarding foreign exchange rates and currency risks apply equally to overseas equities as to overseas bonds.

Derivatives

Active investors who want to profit in the short term, especially when share prices are volatile or on the slide, will find it difficult if invested directly in equities. Shares are a 'long only' investment. You cannot sell a share you do not own with the intention of buying it back later, known as 'going short'.

However, there are financial instruments known as 'derivatives', which make it possible for you to benefit from falling prices. They are called derivatives because they are derived from underlying equities or other securities and include the following:

- options;
- futures;
- warrants;
- contracts for difference;
- spread betting.

Derivatives can usually be purchased for a small percentage only of the cost of a position in the underlying equity itself. They are likely to be even more volatile than the equity on which they are based, with a correspondingly higher potential for loss. They are more like gambling than investing and as a private investor, you should probably leave them well alone. For that reason, I am not going to explain the meaning of each kind of derivative.

Even a private client portfolio, investing directly in equities and managed by a firm of stockbrokers or the like, will probably not include derivatives. However, a professional fund manager running a unit trust or OEIC may use them to some extent to reduce risk.

Hedge funds

A hedge fund is a fund that uses aggressive strategies such as short selling, swaps, arbitrage, derivatives, leverage and program trades. Hedge funds target absolute performance. Their objective is to provide an actual positive return, regardless of whether the market is falling or rising. Again, hedge funds are not for you as a private investor and I will not attempt to explain how any of these techniques or instruments work. Most of them rely on a heavy use of complex mathematical models.

Fund of hedge funds

You could still gain exposure to hedge funds, if they appeal to you, by investing in a fund of hedge funds. This sounds complicated but is simply another kind of collective fund that itself invests in variety of individual hedge funds.

Investing in this way, in a portfolio of unconnected alternative investment strategies has the potential to achieve positive returns within risk boundaries, whatever the position of the underlying stock market may be. Probably the best advice to you or me is 'If you don't understand it, don't do it'.

Checklist

1. Shareholders are at the end of the queue if a company becomes insolvent and its assets are liquidated for distribution.
2. Preference shares are 'preferred' because the company pays interest on them after taxation, before any dividend to ordinary shareholders.
3. Ordinary shares are known as 'equities' and come with voting rights attached. Unless a shareholder or group of shareholders

owns a large proportion of the shares in issue, voting rights do not give any degree of control.

4. Investor rewards come from holding equities until the price appreciates and from dividends that the company pays out. The rewards of equity investment over longer periods can be spectacular. The average return over 20-year periods, after allowing for inflation, has been 8 per cent a year compared with 2 per cent a year for UK government bonds.

5. Portfolio investment spreads the risk of buying shares in specific companies by investing in a range of companies over selected industry sectors.

6. Ask yourself why share tipsters don't follow their own advice and become millionaires.

7. Stock market prices are not just the result of the logical interplay of investment factors. Greed, fear and the herd instinct are the human factors that drive bull markets up and bear markets down.

8. It is sensible to invest in overseas companies through investment trusts or open-ended investment companies (OEICs).

9. Leave derivatives well alone. Even a firm of stockbrokers managing a private client portfolio will probably not include derivatives.

10. Direct investment in hedge funds is also not for you, but you could invest in a fund of hedge funds. But if you don't understand how hedge funds work, your best advice is not to invest in them.

TREND SIGNAL

TRADERS

built for traders by traders

TrendSignal is Trading Software brought to you by professional ex-City traders – People that know the markets and trade them every day.

Four facts you should know about the stock market

FACT 1: You can make money from falling as well as rising prices
FACT 2: You can make money in as little as 10 minutes per day
FACT 3: Trading can generate you a second income
FACT 4: You don't have to be a genius to profit from the stock market

Learn the details of these simple truths and many, many more at one of our FREE introductory seminars.

TrendSignal is designed by 20 year veteran traders and is easy-to-use by novices and professionals alike. TrendSignal is designed to make it easy to spot profitable trading opportunities across all types of financial spread bets – from markets as diverse as shares, stock indices, foreign exchange, commodities and bonds.

TrendSignal is unique. TrendSignal Trading software will help improve your trading performance – If you are just starting out in the exciting world of trading then TrendSignal will give you that confidence to succeed.

BONUS…we now include a FREE full day's trading course (Normal cost £597) with every purchase of TrendSignal.

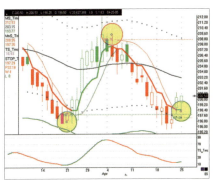

- Successful trading is not down to luck.
- Unlike other people we don't say trading is easy.
- As full time traders we know that to make money you need an edge.
- TrendSignal is our edge – and now you could benefit from it too!

Call 01234 757553 / 020 7060 0467 or visit http://www.trendsignal.co.uk for a brochure and in-depth guide to Financial Spread Betting.

Remember, you can make money when the stock market falls as well as rises. Not just from stocks and shares either. Fed up with rising petrol prices? You wouldn't be if you had made a financial spread bet on the price of oil rising. Don't delay.

Contact us **now** to reserve your place at one of our **FREE** seminars. Places are limited and they are offered on a first come first go basis.

TrendSignal is recommended by:

HandHeldTrades
www.handheldtrades.com

TrendSignal is powered by eSignal.
The provider of affordable, reliable, real-time Market Data

Survive and prosper in Spread Betting

It sounds easy. Many people each year take up financial spread betting, believing that it will be easy, a simple way to supplement their income. Unfortunately, for the majority, it doesn't end up that way.

The percentage of people that lose money spread betting over the medium term is anywhere between 60% and 80%, according to most industry estimates.

The reason? Most punters jump into trading spreads without a clear idea of how they are going to try to beat the markets and without a disciplined approach for limiting their risks.

Remember that when you trade the markets, whether by spread betting, buying and selling futures or any other technique, you will be up against a lot of very clever people, not to mention the world's top investment houses.

You need to have an edge that will give you the chance of profiting in the face of this opposition. Among the 100,000 people in Britain who have financial spread betting accounts, the successful ones have worked out their own method – usually concentrating on a small number of markets; and maintaining a particular style, either based on charting or judgement of the fundamentals.

Done properly, spread betting is a great way to speculate on the markets. It is flexible in that you can trade any market from the one account, it is free of tax and also the paperwork that goes with submitting a tax return, and trades can be made with the click of a mouse.

Making profits also involves being able to close down a loss-making position before it does you too much damage. It always feels horrible to take a loss, but experienced traders will tell you that the negative feeling disappears after a few days.

Crucially, traders who are grown-up enough to take a loss at the right time have the ability to go on and give themselves a chance with a new trade. There is a "traders' trap" – part of human psychology that encourages an individual to stick with a loss-making situation in the hope of a turn-around, or to turn his back on it. That is the route to failure in spread betting, or any other form of short-term investment.

Why are we telling you all of this? At Twowaymarkets Ltd, we offer the best independent advice in the UK to spread betting traders. Our experts, with many years of experience, not only suggest trades based on technical and fundamental analysis but provide ongoing advice on where to place stop-losses and when to take profits.

We are grown-up, and admit when trades have not worked out – something that cannot be said for every advice or training company in this market. We know, and we have no problem in reminding you, that you can't get the gain, without some pain.

What do we offer? First of all, we provide three different advice services for traders – Twowaytrade.com, Onewaybet.com and Handheldtrades.com.

Twowaytrade.com publishes a daily newsletter for experienced investors. This contains in-depth analysis and recommendations on individual UK equities and international stock indices, generated by one of the most sophisticated charting software programmes in use anywhere in the market. Twowaytrade also has a busy desk of advisors, providing telephone advice for traders in contracts for difference (CFDs).

Onewaybet.com is one of the longest established and most popular advice websites for spread betting traders, offering a range of emailed advice services on both individual stocks and the FTSE100 index.

Handheldtrades.com offers an even more convenient distribution method – advice on big financial markets, such as the major US and European stock indices, by text message straight to your mobile phone.

For details on how to get advice from Twowaymarkets Ltd please call **020 7060 0467** or visit **www.twowaytrade.com www.onewaybet.com** or **www.handheldtrades.com**

To open a spread betting account please go directly to **www.twowayspreads.com**

10 Investing wisely

This chapter is intended for those of you who have more than just a few thousand pounds to invest. If you have less than £10,000 you should probably confine your investments to cash deposits or, perhaps, UK government bonds. Only if you have rather more, should you think seriously about investment in equities.

We'll start with an explanation of how to value equities and why you shouldn't trade on the stock market for your own account. We move on to how you can invest in equities without making the selection yourself. Then we'll review the case for consulting an independent financial adviser. Finally, if you feel an irresistible urge to dabble in stocks and shares yourself, you will find some suggestions on learning how to develop informed judgement and the procedures.

How to value equities

So far, we haven't discussed how to decide whether a share represents good value at a certain price or when to buy and when to sell. The share price itself is the most obvious indicator of value. You could say that when a share falls in price it represents better value for money because it costs less and that when a share's price rises, because it costs more, it is less good value. But that is too simple a conclusion. Maybe the change in share price reflects a material change in the value of the company itself – perhaps the directors have announced that the company won't reach its profit forecast in the current year. In that case, there is a very good reason for the share price to fall. Sometimes there is a change in the ownership of the share itself resulting in dilution. For example, if a company has 5,000,000 shares in issue trading at £1 and then issues a further 5,000,000 shares on a one-for-one basis to existing holders (called a 'scrip issue'), the share price should fall to 50p. If it falls to 60p, at the new price the shares are worse value for new shareholders but existing shareholders have made a paper profit.

A valuation yardstick must not be dependent on the share price alone to be useful. There are two ratios that are used most commonly in comparing the share price of a company against the market as a whole or against other companies in the same business sector or having similar characteristics: price earnings ratio and dividend yield; often combined with another ratio: dividend cover.

Price earnings ratio

This ratio is simply earnings per share divided by the price per share, which expresses the concept that a share price can be thought of simply as 'buying the company's earnings'.

Earnings can be calculated in a number of different ways, most commonly either on the basis of the historic audited accounting figures or on forward projections for the current financial year. Broadly, earnings are the profits of a company after taxation and payments to any other class of stock that ranks ahead of the issued ordinary share capital, for example, preference share dividends. Earnings per share are simply the company's earnings divided by the number of shares in issue.

Dividend yield and dividend cover

Dividend yield is simply the dividend per share divided by the share price expressed as a percentage. For example, if the dividend paid or to be paid on a £1 share is 10p and the share price is £2, the dividend yield is 10 divided by 200 × 100 per cent = 5 per cent.

Dividend cover is calculated as the earnings per share, which can be thought of as the profit available for distribution divided by the dividend paid per share. In the above example if the earnings per share were 20p then the dividend cover would be 20p divided by 10p = 2. If a company maintains a similar dividend cover from year to year, there is no cause for concern. If the dividend cover falls in order to maintain the dividend, there may be a question mark over future performance.

Both price earnings ratio and dividend yield coupled with dividend cover need to be compared against some benchmark to give a view of the value of the share at its current price. The benchmark could be an index of historic performance of the market overall, such as the FTSE 100 (an index of share prices of the top 100 companies listed on the London Stock

Exchange). Alternatively, the current price earnings ratios and dividend yields of comparable companies generally provide a better benchmark.

Historic comparisons are only enlightening as long as you believe that history will repeat itself or have a clear idea of how it will differ from the past. Comparisons with similar companies are likely to be of more value in assessing current value. A share with a price earnings ratio of 10 will be cheaper than one with a ratio of 15 and a share yielding 5 per cent will be dearer than one yielding 10 per cent if dividend cover is considered adequate in both cases.

Why investing on a stock market for yourself is hazardous

You will have read enough by now to realize that prudent investment in equities demands not just a thorough understanding of how stock markets react but careful research into the past and present performance of different industry sectors and individual shares. Such research will give you some basis for forecasting what is likely to happen both in the short term and over the longer periods during which you are advised to hold equity investments. The experience and time commitment you will have to make to manage equity investment yourself is considerable. Without that attention to detail any investment that you manage yourself in equities is reduced to a gamble.

It is human nature to go for quick gains but that is not what investing in equities is about. Many amateurs follow a strategy of selling shares that show a decent profit and hanging on to those that do badly in the hope that 'something will turn up', which makes them winners. Investment guru Jim Slater, who is still on top form at age 75, advises the opposite. Run with shares that have done well over a period and sell quickly those that perform badly is the order of his day. In the context of holding investments over a period of 20 years or more, the advice makes sense. Jim Slater once asked the question 'Would you put your small change in a pocket with a hole in it?' and that is a good way to think of shares that are losers. Mr Slater has consistently followed his own advice and is a wealthy man.

If you are fortunate enough to have quite a large sum of money to invest, at least £20,000, you would need to decide what your investment policy should be in terms of where to put your money. Most investment experts would suggest a conventional balance of investments such as the following:

■ 50 per cent in secure investments – fixed income deposits, bonds (and perhaps property rentals);
■ 40 per cent in medium-risk investments, such as FTSE 100 tracker funds (described below);
■ 10 per cent in high risk investments such as equities.

Of course, the proportions can be adjusted to suit your personal attitude towards risk.

Although the high risk proportion to be invested in equities is relatively small, the same experts would caution you strongly against undertaking the investment yourself. You do not have to get involved in the complex research of investment factors outlined above or to worry about the fads and fashions of market sentiment. Instead, you can either put your money into funds such as investment trusts or open-ended investment companies (OEICs), managed by investment professionals or appoint a professional investment adviser to manage your investments.

Trading on the stock market, defined as the buying and selling of stocks and shares for short-term profits is far more hazardous and should be avoided unless you have had expert training.

Investing in funds

Investment funds are offered by unit trusts, investment trusts and OEICs in shares, corporate bonds, gilts, deposits and other investments. Professional managers select the investments they think will do best and switch from one to the other according to changing market conditions.

The following types of fund are identified by the Financial Services Authority (FSA) as the better known among a wide variety that you might consider suitable for your investment:

■ *Money market* Invested in deposits. These are low risk funds but cannot be expected to give you high returns in the long run.
■ *Bond-based* Invested in corporate bonds, gilts and/or similar stocks. They are medium to low risk and normally aim at providing income rather than growth.

▌ *General* Invested in a wide range of investments. They can be aimed at providing income or growth (or both) and are suitable for those who want a medium-risk investment.

▌ *Tracker* Unlike other funds in this list, there is no fund manager actively choosing and switching stocks. The investments are organized to move in line with a selected stock market index – such as the FTSE 100. Charges are usually lower because there's no active management. Of course, without active management your investment will follow the index to which it is tied slavishly, with no opportunity to switch when the index suffers a downturn. Even high street banks offer stock market linked growth bonds. The HSBC bond available from 24 January to 8 April 2005 was designed to return 100 per cent of any percentage rise of the FTSE 100 index (after allowing for averaging), subject to a maximum return of 50 per cent of your initial investment and repayment of the original investment after five years.

▌ *Property* Invested directly in commercial property (such as offices) and shopping centres and/or in the shares of property companies.

▌ *Specialist* Invested in a particular sector, such as Japan, or particular kinds of shares such as small companies. Suitable only if you are willing to accept the higher risk.

▌ *Ethical* Either general or specialist funds, but some types of investment (for example, shares in defence companies) are excluded and others (such as shares in companies with good employment practices) are actively selected. If you have an interest in ethical funds, you can find more information by contacting the Ethical Research Services Centre on (020) 7840 5700 or on their website www. eiris.org.

How unit trust and OEIC funds work

Unit trusts work by taking your money and placing it in a fund, together with money from other investors. The fund invests on your behalf in the stock market, government bonds, property, cash and other investments, depending on the type of unit trust that you have chosen. Your money remains in the fund for as long as you hold your 'units' in the trust.

OEICs and unit trusts operate in similar ways. In each case, the fund is divided into units. There is no limit to the number of units you can buy and each unit is of equal value. The value of the units is the value of the underlying investments that produce returns for the overall fund. The number of units you own determines your share of the overall return. Both unit trusts and OEICs are available as products within an ISA wrapper (see Chapter 6) or as products without the benefits of that tax treatment.

Investment trusts

Investment trusts are companies that invest in the shares of other companies. As with any other shares, there is a small bid/offer spread with all investment trust shares traded on the stock exchange (the dealers do have to make a living!). However, the bid/offer spread is not as wide as the 5 per cent that is the norm with most unit trusts.

Investment trust shares are often said to be 'at a discount'. This means that the current share price is lower than the net asset value (NAV) per share; in other words the present sales value of all the shares held in other companies divided by the number of shares in the investment trust. Some investment trusts borrow money against the value of their holdings to invest in more shares. Such investment trusts are said to be 'geared'.

You can hold your investment trust shares in an ISA, which will give you the same tax advantages as unit trusts, which may also be held in an ISA wrapper.

Definitions of fund sectors

The trade body representing UK unit trust and fund managers is the Investment Management Association (IMA), which groups all authorized unit trust and OIEC funds into sectors. The sectors are divided into growth funds and income funds and are listed by the IMA as follows:

Growth funds
■ *UK All Companies* Funds that invest at least 80 per cent of their assets in UK equities having capital growth as their main objective.
■ *Europe Excluding UK* Funds that invest at least 80 per cent of their assets in European securities and exclude UK equities.
■ *Balanced Managed* Funds that offer investment in a range of assets. At least 10 per cent must be held in non-UK equities. Assets must be at least 50 per cent in sterling/euro and are deemed to include convertibles.

▌ *Global Growth* Funds that invest at least 80 per cent of their assets in equities but not more than 80 per cent in UK assets, and have the prime object of achieving capital growth.

Income funds

▌ *UK Corporate Bond* Funds that invest at least 80 per cent of their assets in sterling-denominated (or hedged bank deposits), Triple BBB minus or above bonds as measured by either Standard & Poor's or equivalent (Moody's Baa or above) or convertibles.

▌ *UK Other Bond* Funds investing at least 80 per cent of their assets in sterling-denominated (or hedged back to sterling) bonds and 20 per cent of their assets in below Triple BBB minus bonds as measured by either Standard & Poor's or equivalent, or preference shares.

There are many sub-varieties of growth and income funds and also some specialist funds that you will find listed on the consumer section of the FSA website at www.fsa.gov.uk.

Financial advisers

Financial advisers who give advice on most kinds of investment and the companies they work for must be authorized by the FSA and must follow the rules designed to protect their customers.

About the only kind of investment product on which advisers do not have to be FSA authorized yet are equity release schemes (reversion schemes) other than mortgages. It is expected that they will also be authorized by the FSA within two years. In fact, the distinction between independent financial advisers (IFAs) and tied agents is set to be removed shortly.

To find out whether an adviser or the company they represent is fully authorized, telephone the FSA Consumer Contact Centre Helpline on (0845) 606 1234 for that information.

Paying for financial advice

Financial advisers are generally paid by:

▌ commission, usually a percentage taken out of the money you pay or invest; or

▌ one-off fee, usually paid direct to the adviser; or
▌ a combination of commission and fee.

Since the middle of 2004, investment advisers wishing to call themselves 'independent' must give you the option, if you prefer, to pay by fee.

If you pay an adviser by commission, you pay for the advice through the product charges. You should take into account that often the charges are the same, whether you buy through an adviser or not.

Always ask a financial adviser before you make a commitment how much the fees are and how they are to be paid. Some advisers will give you back part of the commission if you ask. In this way, you may still get the advice and a cheaper, improved product.

The following are some recommendations of how to engage with financial advisers:

▌ Check whether the investment adviser is authorized.
▌ Check carefully whether you are being given advice or information. If you know the particular product you want to buy, check out whether you can buy it cheaper through an adviser or direct from the supplier.
▌ Always take accurate notes when you meet an adviser. Ask for a copy of the fact find and your completed application form. These are all essential in case of a dispute or compensation claim later.
▌ Make sure you understand all documents. If you don't, ask. Don't be embarrassed to ask questions.
▌ Shop around and compare different products to ensure that you are getting best value. Don't be fooled by promises of amazing deals.
▌ Don't be afraid to say 'no', even if the adviser has been recommended by a friend or you don't want to disappoint them.
▌ Never sign anything until you are confident that you understand it and never sign a blank form allowing the adviser to fill in the details later.
▌ Think twice before signing anything.

Financial advice and your legal rights

For some types of financial products, either the law or non-statutory codes of practice may give you certain rights and protection when you use an adviser. However, you often lose some of these rights if you buy without advice.

Don't mistake information for advice. You usually buy without advice if you invest through a direct offer advertisement, such as a mailshot or invest through a direct offer company or on the internet, and sometimes without advice when you buy a stakeholder pension.

When you base your buying decision on information printed in a mailshot, or on a website, you have the right to expect the information to be accurate and complete. Information that turns out to have been wrong or misleading gives you the right to complain and seek compensation for any resulting loss.

Do it yourself

If you are still attracted to the idea of managing your own stock market investments after all that you have read so far, at least develop your knowledge about investing before you start. A good way to do this is to attend a course organized by a leading investment training specialist, where you can learn more from experts in the business about the many different types of investment available. Some of these regular events provide free education to private investors about a number of ways that they can invest in the world's stock market, property or other alternative investments.

Among the reputable firms that specialize in investment training, Self-Investments Ltd, offers free introductory courses and may be found by visiting its website www.self-investment.com or calling freephone 0808 1431082.

Balanced portfolio investment

You may want to build up a range of investments (a portfolio) with the idea of spreading your risks. Investing through unit OEICs and investment trusts is a good way of taking a portfolio approach, particularly for those with limited capital. You can choose a mixture of high risk and medium risk OEICs and investment trusts or you may prefer to avoid higher risk investment altogether. You can also take a basic decision on the balance you want to achieve between income and capital growth.

In any case, you will want to understand the different levels of risk that each kind of investment described in this chapter offers. You need to know if your money will be invested in a special sector. For example, some unit trusts and investment trusts specialize in sectors, such as energy, technology, pharmaceuticals or small companies. You should also check in what parts of the world your money will be invested. The OEIC or investment trust in which you buy shares might place some or all of your investment in Europe, the United States or the Far East. You need to feel comfortable with how your investment has been dispersed.

Lump sum investment vs. monthly saving

In Chapter 5 you were advised to assess your net income availability before engaging in any form of monthly savings commitment and the same is true of investment. Even if you have only £25 a month to invest, you can gain the advantages of risk spreading by making a regular commitment to buy units in a collective investment. You would also avoid direct dealing costs and time-consuming administration. However, there are some disadvantages too. Any collective investment scheme includes charges for a fund manager's fees and you have absolutely no say in the choice of individual shares or bonds that the manager chooses. Really, as a small monthly investor there is little opportunity for you to invest in individual bonds or equities direct, where dealing charges and administration would be disproportionately high.

Perhaps, the best solution for you, if you want to invest direct but don't have a lump sum at this moment, is to build up a lump sum first through regular monthly payments into a deposit or savings account. You can then withdraw at intervals and place your investments.

Checklist

1. The two most commonly used measures for comparing a share's price against the market or other similar companies are price earnings ratio and dividend yield. Dividend yield is often used together with another ratio, dividend cover.
2. The performance of comparable companies is a better benchmark than historic performance of the company itself or the market.
3. The time commitment you would have to make to manage equity investment effectively yourself is considerable. Without attention to detail any equity investment that you make is more like gambling.

4. Equity investment is for the longer term. Most investment experts would suggest that you invest no more than 10 per cent of your capital in equities. Understand balanced portfolio investment.

5. Unit trusts and open-ended investment trusts (OEICs) offer you a wide variety of investment funds in shares, corporate bonds, gilts and deposits. Funds are classified into income funds that are focused on producing income and growth funds that concentrate on growth with lower income.

6. The value of the units is the value of the underlying investments that produce return for the overall fund in which you share, according to the number of units you purchase.

7. Nearly all financial advisers and their companies must be authorized by the Financial Services Authority. Check with the FSA Contact Centre that any financial adviser you might appoint is registered.

8. Financial advisers are paid by commission deducted from what you pay or fees. Some advisers will give you back part of the commission if you ask. Independent financial advisers must give you the option to pay fees rather than commission.

9. The law or codes of practice may give you certain rights and protection when you use an adviser. If you buy without advice, you often lose some of these rights.

10. If you really want to manage your stock market investments yourself, at least develop your knowledge about investing by attending an introductory course organized by investment specialists.

Part Five
Active investment

Not the house guests you were expecting?

Would you risk the biggest investment decision of your life by getting only half the story?

Over 400,000 properties are built on rubbish, more than 320,000 are close to chemical-release sites and over 2 million are at risk from flooding – but this won't be obvious from the house details or surveyors report. What about mobile phone masts, neighbourhood crime and planning applications that could also affect your property's value?

Homecheck has helped millions of homebuyers uncover the facts about environmental and planning risks. We provide a comprehensive assessment from just £29, giving you the heads up on vital information that could affect your purchase decision. You can get these from your solicitor, or via our nationwide network of resellers. A free on-line service is also available for you to get an overview of your postcode. For more information visit us at **www.homecheck.co.uk** or call us on **0870 606 1700**.

Don't buy a home without us.

Should your new home carry a wealth warning?

Picture the scene – you've just completed on your dream property or somewhere you know would be a great buy to let investment opportunity and you find out that that it was built on a landfill site forty years ago. What's worse, there's nothing you can do about it – the house could be blighted and you may end up having to foot the bill for any clean up work that is required.

Protecting yourself with the right searches

Your solicitor may only conduct a "local authority search" which seeks to find answers to any planning, drainage or water issues within the boundary or immediate area adjacent to the house you are thinking of buying. This doesn't go far enough to assess what other environmental issues could be present and there could be a nasty surprise just 100 meters away!

You should ensure a thorough environmental and planning report is undertaken to ensure your investment is sound. It is essential that you insist that your solicitor makes these enquiries and obtains environmental and planning information specific to your property and nearby area.

What risks do you need to think about?

Contamination: Your property could be built on an area once occupied by heavy industry. It could have been a garage, where diesel tanks could have leaked into the ground, or a factory where chemicals were stored in a way that was far less controlled than today. Toxic substances like cadmium, arsenic and lead have all been used in the past and often have leaked into the soil, to remain active for hundreds of years.

What happens if you extend the property and uncover these toxins? Legislation in place states that you, not the local authority, would have to pay a bill that could run into tens of thousands of pounds.

Flooding: What if your ground floor was flooded, with no or limited protection from your house insurance policy? You may not know from your insurance company before it's too late.

Subsidence: Past deep mining activity and, more importantly, shallow mines for tin, copper and gravel could have significant effects on the stability of your property – what if a hole appears adjacent to your house requiring underpinning and extensive, structural repair?

How common are environmental risks?

These are some figures you should think about:

- Over 400,000 homes in the UK are close to a landfill site with increasing concern that they could pose a health hazard to those living near them.
- More than 2 million homes are at risk from flooding. Floods like those experienced in Boscastle, Carlisle and York are becoming increasingly common and the pressure to build on flood plains becomes ever more intense.
- Over 320,000 homes are within 5km of a chemical release site. Major industrial sites nationwide are principally responsible for thousands of tonnes of chemicals discharged to the atmosphere every year.

Where can you get the information you need?

A valuable resource is Homecheck, from Landmark Information Group, which has helped millions of customers, via their solicitor, assess potential environmental impacts on properties nationwide. You can access a FREE overview of potential risks by visiting www.homecheck.co.uk . This is based on a search of your postcode and is designed to indicate possible issues for further investigation.

If something is highlighted, Landmark can provide a full environmental report in more depth and specific to your property, backed by a professional assessment from environmental consultants. You can buy this via your solicitor or by calling direct on 0870 606 1700. Reports cost from just £29 – a small price to pay to protect your investment.

_11_ Hands-on investments

So far we've considered only those financial investments that are on offer to you through banks, building societies and other financial institutions, authorized financial advisers, even through stores or advertised in the newspapers. Once you have taken the decision to save or invest in any of these products, there's nothing for you to do except check their progress regularly and sell them when you are advised to or when you think that the time is right. Your role is not an active one.

You may not find a passive role very satisfying and in this part of the book we turn to investments where you can play an active decision-making role in the management of your investment. Such investments fall generally into one of two categories: hands-on investments, where your money is invested in business assets and you can exercise varying degrees of control, with or without professional advisers, over the management of your investment; and investments in non-business assets related to pastimes and hobbies where you have a keen interest and you yourself are the main decision-maker.

In this chapter we take an overview of just a few kinds of hands-on investment:

- property in the United Kingdom;
- overseas property;
- forestry holdings;
- business angel investing.

Of course, there are many more. For example, you might decide to open a shop or a health or garden centre, which you would manage yourself, or a speciality mail order business, or a computer software consultancy. All of these would require a day-to-day management involvement. For the purposes of this chapter 'hands-on' does not mean 'immersed in' and I have deliberately chosen asset-based businesses in which you can be an active decision-maker without being an operating manager.

We explore the second kind of investment in non-business assets in Chapter 12. These are personal investments in which you may already have a keen interest yourself and to succeed you will have to become knowledgeable as well as enthusiastic. I have called them collectively 'A little of what you fancy'.

Property investment in the United Kingdom

Over the years, the returns from property investment have outperformed those of the other asset classes that you read about in Part 4 within the financial investment categories. More recently, UK investors have done very well in the residential buy-to-let market and are now in the commercial property market through various investment vehicles. Cordea Savills, the property fund management specialist, forecast in 2004 that the commercial property market would deliver returns of 9.8 per cent a year for the period 2004 to 2008.

Commercial property

Institutional investors own a large part of UK commercial property, estimated recently at £105 billion by Investment Property Databank. The strong UK landlord and tenant legislation, where tenants often sign long leases of 15 years or more with upward-only rent review clauses, gives the assurance of a known income from a tenant over quite a long period. This feature of the market alone makes investment in commercial property attractive. Even better, commercial property tenancies in the United Kingdom are commonly signed with clauses included that commit the tenant to maintaining the quality of the building they have leased. These Fully Repairing and Insuring (FRI) leases, as they are known, help to minimize the landlord's management and financial risk.

The same advantages apply to private investors buying commercial property in the United Kingdom, provided that you can be sure of finding a tenant and that you only sign leases with fully commercial terms and conditions.

Buying commercial property in continental Europe is altogether more hazardous. Lease terms vary widely from country to country and in some cases are drafted firmly in favour of the tenant at the expense of the landlord. Therefore, if you are thinking of buying commercial property to let as an investment, say a shop or small office building, you are strongly advised to stick to the United Kingdom.

Buy-to-let residential property

Private investors generally favour residential property over commercial property as an investment. This is entirely understandable since their previous experience of investing in property is probably based on successful investment in their own homes.

Until the last quarter of 2004, there was a strong bull market in house prices both for owner occupation and as buy-to-let investments. With low interest rates, cheap buy-to-let loans were available and there were strong markets for student accommodation and seniors' housing so that a steady, continuing increase in capital values seemed assured. Since then, the residential property sector has slowed down while interest rates have risen. However, a modest increase in house prices is forecast by many property professionals later in 2005.

Although the present market is less sparkling there are niche sectors of the buy-to-let market that you might want to consider. One of these is managed student halls where there are opportunities to enter into leases of 20 years or more to universities themselves, sometimes at indexed rents (for example, the rent rises automatically in line with the Retail Price Index). Alternatively, a strong market for short lets to students direct seems a relatively safe bet in light of student numbers expected to rise from 150,000 to 250,000 by 2010.

Another variation on the buy-to-let theme, although hardly hands-on, are the hotel investments offered by GuestInvest in their growing chain of hotels. Investors are offered the opportunity to own a room in an award-winning hotel and to receive 45–50 per cent of the room's income. They also have the option to take up to 52 nights accommodation a year for themselves for £15 to £20 per night as a part of the deal. Investors who bought rooms at Guesthouse West, Notting Hill, London are earning a 7 per cent return on their investment and, after four months can already realize a 10 per cent gain on resale. These investments qualify for inclusion in a SIPP.

Residential property development

During periods of rising property prices, if you have the flair and necessary skills, buying a house in a run-down condition, modernizing and refurbishing it before reselling it can be a very profitable occupation. A second home mortgage will fund most of the initial investment. Of course, the profit you make on resale will be subject to capital gains tax (CGT).

However, if you repeat the process and continue to buy houses for improvement and resale, the Inland Revenue are likely to regard your activity as trading and the profits will be taxed as income. You may be able to avoid CGT by living in the house while you carry out the improvements and nominating it as your principal place of residence (PPR) until it is sold. That may work well the first time, but if you continue to do this, moving into each house as you buy it for the renovation period, your activity is still likely to be treated as one that generates trading income.

If you are more adventurous, or have already succeeded in developing land that you own, you might decide to buy a house with a large garden or paddock attached where you believe that there is a good opportunity of gaining planning consent to build more housing units. There are no certainties in planning applications and, if you agree a price subject to planning consent before buying, the price will reflect the development value. There are big profits to be made in buying development property before planning consent but you need to be particularly skilled and experienced in planning applications yourself to limit the risk. Alternatively, you could go into partnership with a local builder who has previous experience of the planning officer and local authority planning committee and knows how they are likely to decide on your application.

If all of this seems too much and you decide that direct investment in property is not for you, you can always resort to buying shares in a quoted property or real estate company with a good track record. For an indirect involvement in residential property you can buy shares in a company that is a house builder itself or supplies materials for building houses. You could also buy shares (or units) in a collective investment vehicle such as an OEIC or unit trust that specializes in investing in property.

These collective investment vehicles are not quite as flexible as those that invest in stocks and shares where the fund manager can respond to heavy sales of units by selling off underlying investment quickly – it takes longer to sell off underlying properties. Therefore, the OEICs and unit trusts invested in property may have restricted dealing periods and may be priced at infrequent intervals.

ALLIED
SURVEYORS

Allied Surveyors is one of the UK's largest independent firms of Chartered Surveyors providing genuine postcode coverage throughout England, Wales, Scotland and N. Ireland. Our teams of experienced Chartered Surveyors provide professional property advice to major lending institutions, companies and private individuals.

We recognise that buying your home is probably the biggest purchase that you will make in your lifetime and so you need some assurance that you are making a good decision. Before making that final offer and agreeing to purchase the home of your dreams, we would strongly recommend that you obtain an independent survey of the property.

The surveyor will establish whether the asking price is fair and also help identify any pitfalls. This will not only help you find out whether you are paying the right price but may also offer some bargaining power for you to renegotiate the price.

We provide the full range of reports and surveys including;

Valuation Report
This is a brief report in respect of value only. You will need a valuation if you wish to get a mortgage but it can also be used for a variety of purposes including mortgage security, taxation, probate and family issues.

RICS Homebuyer Survey and Valuation (often simply referred to as an HSV)
This is an economy service for purchasers, devised by the Royal Institution of Chartered Surveyors, and involves a more detailed inspection and report than a valuation. It does not go into as much detail as a full Building Survey but is nonetheless generally considered suitable for modern traditional properties and will comment on the general condition of all visible sections of the property.

Home Condition Survey
This is a report developed by Allied Surveyors and is designed to

highlight significant defects whilst reporting in a concise user friendly format. All accessible parts of the building will be inspected and the report will include any required action points needed to retain the saleability of the property. If requested, it can also include an Energy Efficiency Rating for the property and a full Security Report.

This report is therefore beneficial to both purchasers and sellers. Prospective purchasers can feel confident that they can use this report to assist in making a reasoned and informed judgement on whether or not to proceed with the purchase, and sellers may benefit as pre-sale surveys can help to speed up the whole buying and selling process.

Building Survey – sometimes referred to as a structural survey
This is the most detailed and comprehensive type of report available and is particularly suitable for older buildings which are more likely to have something wrong with them. It is also ideal for unusual style properties, large buildings, or those which have been extended.

Energy Efficiency and Security Reports
Allied Surveyors can also provide full Energy Efficiency and Security Reports on the property. An Energy Report will give advice on how to upgrade to achieve greater fuel efficiency as well as providing an energy rating assessment.

As concern continues to mount over rising crime figures, the Allied Surveyors Security Report provides information relating to the vulnerability of the property to intrusion. It looks at the adequacy of door and window locks together with other security measures including intruder alarms and makes recommendations for any required improvements.

For further advise and guidance on which type of report would suit your needs please visit our website **www.alliedsurveyors.com** or alternatively call our client services team on **08700 740750**.

It is also worth bearing in mind that we have very high standards of quality and have Quality Assurance through Lloyd's Register Quality Assurance (LRQA) to standard ISO9001:2000.

Gill Hall BSc (Hons) DMS
Business Development Director

advertisement feature

The simple way to wet room creation

Stylish and spacious, wet rooms are fast becoming the popular choice for discerning property developers and owners. The versatility offered by a wet room provides an unrivalled space in which creativity can be unleashed.

Now, transforming existing or new traditional style bathrooms into a modern wet room has become simple, fast and effective with a complete package solution from CCL Specialist Supplies Limited. Comprising a preformed shower base, superior quality waterproof membrane and drain fitting, the package provides everything required to create the perfect wet room area with reduced installation time.

Suitable for most types of bathroom with timber or concrete floors, the preformed shower base, with a depth of 22mm, is engineered for maximum durability and high performance. The preformed gradients ensure that all water flows efficiently to the drain and eliminate the need to notch out joists.

In addition to the shower base, the Tilesafe membrane has also been designed for simple installation. This high quality self-adhesive waterproofing material is supplied at a size of 10m², sufficient for covering most shower areas. Compatible with all quality adhesives, the membrane can be fixed to ply, masonry, concrete or plasterboard to form a secure internal watertight structure.

Since wet rooms offer the opportunity to create the ultimate in bathroom design, CCL Specialist Supplies also provides a choice of drain fitting finishes to complement the style of the room.

Simplicity and versatility are the key attributes of a wet room, and so too for the complete solution from CCL Specialist Supplies. With reduced installation times and the flexibility to use the products in almost any situation, the creation of the perfect wet room is easily achieved with this simple, robust solution.

For a brochure or more information, telephone **01256 763 100**
or visit our website **www.tile-safe.co.uk**

Fortunately, the government has introduced in 2004 a new collective investment vehicle, called a Property Investment Fund, modelled on a highly successful US equivalent and existing offshore quoted closed-end trusts, in which shares can be bought and sold as easily as any other unit trust or OEIC.

Overseas property

You may already have been put off the idea of investing directly in property overseas by horror stories about investors in Spain finding that they do not have a protected freehold title to the properties they have bought, or second home buyers in France who renovate their houses to a high standard and are then charged an 'improvement' tax.

Buy-to-let opportunities

If you are still attracted to the idea of a 'buy-to-let' investment in continental Europe or further afield, you should first understand that market conditions are very different from those in the United Kingdom. For example, you may be surprised to find that deposits on new properties are much higher than in the United Kingdom (typically 20 to 30 per cent) because they are often used by the seller to fund the building cost. In some countries, such as Turkey, the rules for foreigners regarding land title are such that it is not possible for you to raise a mortgage. In fact, the 'buy-to-let' mortgage is still almost unknown outside the United Kingdom, although there is evidence that the international banks are beginning to move into country-specific mortgage and other finance products.

Another hazard is the varying levels of consumer protection. Overseas consumer law will not protect you after you have signed a contract as it will in the United Kingdom. You need to be absolutely sure that you are buying through a reputable professional firm of estate agents. It is a good idea to work through a reputable company in the United Kingdom that has done the local market research and has the network in place to help you where you want to go. This kind of advice won't be cheap but it is better to pay for it from an independent firm on a 'time spent' basis than to rely on the 'free' advice of an intermediary acting for the seller. This will also give you the possibility of redress if you find out later that you have been misled.

It's about time the Government gave investors something to smile about!

For your free guide to Landbanking call:
020 7242 4242

Plot Your Path To Riches

Mark Twain famously said "Buy land – they're not making any more of it" and this is certainly true, with the exception of reclamation projects and other schemes. In England, a densely populated country, we need all the building land that we can get. The mounting pressure to provide land to meet the insatiable demand for new houses has resulted in stratospheric increases in the price of land. House prices are the main topic of conversation across every dinner table in the country – but few people realize that although property prices have increased by an average of just over 300% over the last 20 years, land has shot up by over 800% over the same period (according to figures published by the Halifax).

For generations, landowners and the house-building industry has exploited the future potential of land by buying sites for their strategic value in years to come, sites perhaps on the fringes of existing conurbations, where there is no current likelihood for planning permission, but where an informed opinion feels there is a good chance of planning permission being granted at some future stage. This concept of buying land with a view to profit from the increase in value that comes with re-zoning, or change of use, is known as Landbanking.

Landbanking has, until recently, been the sole preserve of house-builders and landowners with deep pockets. It is they that have had the resources to hunt for suitable sites and employ the army of professionals – planning consultants, solicitors, surveyors, architects, and so on – required to take such projects through to fruition. Although the costs involved can be staggering, with the right expertise at your disposal, the rewards can be astonishing: agricultural land can be bought for as little as £10,000 per hectare, yet that same piece of land, once residential planning permission has been granted, could sell for £2 million (the average price for an hectare of development land in the UK).

Until recently, the problem for private investors has been this: how does one take advantage of the huge opportunities that land offers without spending inordinate amounts of time and money getting in the game? Now, European Land Sales Partnership and its associates have developed a perfect solution for private investors who want to enter this lucrative market.

The team features partner John Beckwith-Smith, an award-winning civil engineer and planning professional, and associate Jerry Smith, Director of Parkhall Estates, a firm of property development consultants that have acted an behalf of the country's leading house-builders for over a decade. The team is committed to making available to individual buyers the opportunity to purchase strategic plots of land . Uniquely, the price paid for each plot has the costs associated with gaining planning factored in, so that once a purchase has been made, no further calls are made upon the plotholder. This offers investors a stress-free and affordable entry into the world of landbanking.

The UK is currently suffering from a chronic housing shortage due to demographic changes such as increased single occupancy homes, life longevity and immigration. The Deputy Prime Minister, John Prescott, recently announced far-reaching measures to address the issue, and the UK Government is now highly committed to building millions of new homes across the UK to help ease the crisis. This will involve re-zoning many hectares of land, converting fields, that historically could not be built on, into prime development sites. This, in turn, is providing astute investors with an opportunity to make substantial profits from owning a solid asset.

To take advantage yourself, contact European Land Sales Partnership for a free consultation on **020 7242 4242**. Plot prices begin at a surprisingly affordable £3000.

In the same way, always use a lawyer who is an overseas specialist and who is governed by the Law Society. You will have recognized in advance of your purchase that managing your property, when it becomes yours, is much harder and more time-consuming at a distance and involves all kinds of local regulations of which you may be completely unaware. The sensible way to deal with the problems of filing returns, getting tenants, maintenance and emergency repairs is to employ a 'turnkey' service, a locally-based provider with experienced staff that will carry out all these tasks for a percentage of the rental income.

Overseas property investments

There are opportunities to participate in overseas property development on a syndicated basis where the individual's investment can be as little as £15,000. Investors can invest in any part of the value chain arising from the development of quality property in premium locations. The stages at which you can invest range from financing overseas developments, through providing seed capital for new developments to buying completed units.

Of course, you need to be very careful in your selection of the specialist development company with which you place your investment, but there are reputable developers with good track records that you can consult, such as Stop Think Investment Group.

Forestry investment

Unlike other types of investment studied in this chapter, forestry investment relies on organic physical growth for its financial returns. Trees grow. In the United Kingdom, commercial conifers grow at a rate of about 4 to 5 per cent each year over the life of the crop. With skilful buying, careful management and well-timed harvesting, the financial returns can be improved up to 8 to 10 per cent a year tax-free.

You have probably heard of the Forestry Commission, which is the dominant player in the British forestry industry, but more than half of Britain's commercial forests are owned by institutions or private investors. Planned, financially-driven investment by wealthy individuals took centre stage during the high-taxation decades of the 1960s, 1970s and 1980s.

Wish you could check how much you could save by switching your mortgage rate?

The Remortgage Index identifies potential

**First year savings on £100,000 mortgage = £1,740*

YOUR MOVE
REMORTGAGE INDEX

08000 153 800

Think carefully before securing other debts against your home. Your home may be repossessed if you do not keep up repayments on your mortgage.

YOUR MOVE

BUYING A PROPERTY? –NEED TO REMORTGAGE?

The subject of remortgaging is now becoming a major talking point in the media and it's not surprising when you consider the mortgage repayment reductions that could be made when switching to a new lender or to a new deal.

Understanding the many different mortgages available, however, can be a confusing business unless you take professional advice.

It's often not quite as simple as choosing the lender who is offering the lowest interest rate at the time. You also need to think about other factors such as: Do you plan to move again soon? Do you want your repayments to remain fixed? Do you want your repayments to stay below a certain interest rate? All of which could make a big difference to the amount you pay in the short and long term.

There are basically two ways to set up a mortgage: Repayment or Interest only.

REPAYMENT MORTGAGES
With a repayment mortgage you pay part interest and part capital repayments to the lender each month and in this way the capital debt outstanding is reduced until the loan is repaid.

INTEREST ONLY MORTGAGES
With an interest only mortgage it is usual to have use an investment vehicle in place to repay the loan at the end of the mortgage term and in the meantime interest is paid to the lender on the outstanding balance. The debt remains the same while the value of the investment should increase, usually over a specified term, when the value should equal or exceed the original debt. However, there is a risk that the value of the investment vehicle may not be enough to repay the debt at the end of the mortgage term.

Some lenders are able to offer a combination of the above methods which may be more suited to your individual circumstances.

WHAT TYPE OF INTEREST RATE MAY BE AVAILABLE?
In addition to the standard variable interest rate, there are many different schemes available: Fixed, Discount, Tracker, Capped, Cap and collar and Cashback or even a combination of some of the above.

VARIABLE RATES
This is probably the most common type of loan. The interest rate that you are charged goes up and down in line with interest rates in the economy as a whole. When interest rates go up, the amount that you have to pay usually also rises, and payments can fall when interest rates come down. A good example of a type of rate that falls into this category is a "Tracker" rate see below.

FIXED RATES

The rate is fixed for a specified number of years, so you know what your payments will be over that period. Following this period, the rate will usually revert to the lender's standard variable rate. Special fixed rate schemes are often available for first time buyers.

CAPPED RATES

This has similar advantages to a fixed rate as the interest rate will not rise above the 'cap' for a pre-determined period. These schemes may sometimes include a 'collar' or minimum rate level which is the level the rate will not fall below.

DISCOUNTED RATES

A discounted rate gives you a reduction of, for example, 2% off the lenders standard variable rate for a specified period. So, although the rate may still rise and fall, you will be paying less than the standard variable rate.

FLEXIBLE MORTGAGES

A more recent innovation, these can give various benefits which usually include the ability to vary monthly payments in line with your changing circumstances. They may also allow you to take 'payment holidays' and to borrow back any overpayment you have made.

TRACKER

Popular with more sophisticated buyers, the rate is set as a % above base rate (often with a discount period as an added attraction to customers) and will move in line with Bank of England base rate.

CASHBACK

After the mortgage completes an agreed figure is paid to the mortgagee. (i.e. £500) Useful for First Time Buyers but can often have an impact through an extended tie in period or early redemption penalties.

Whatever mortgage you eventually choose it's wise to make sure you've got the advice and guidance of a reputable financial advisor especially one who is able to advise you when your existing 'deal' may be coming to an end. Remortgaging needn't be such a daunting prospect and with the right advice could present a great way of reducing your monthly outgoings and save you significant amounts in the long run.

YOUR MOVE is a trading name of: your-move.co.uk Limited which is authorised and regulated by the Financial Services Authority (FRN:310467) for mortgages and non-investment insurance advice.

Registered Office Address: Newcastle House, Albany Court, Newcastle Business Park, Newcastle upon Tyne, NE4 7YB.   Registered Number: 01864469.   VAT Number GB842795983

Plantations are bought and sold at all stages of their development from cleared land to mature forests. They vary in size and value from a few acres worth perhaps £30,000 to thousands of acres worth several millions. Buyers range from pension funds and large insurance companies to wealthy individuals and small investors.

The forestry market

The typical forestry cycle lasts about 40 years, divided into three distinct phases:

- *Early growth years* Owners invest their surplus income so that the young crop is fully established within 7 to 15 years depending on location.
- *Steady capital growth* Minimum intervention and low maintenance costs for 15 to 25 years.
- *Harvesting* Except for very small plantations, harvesting will probably be spread over 5 to 15 years.

In the case of really large properties planting can be staggered so that the three phases of development are all represented and income production is continuous. Forestry professionals would consider this a 'normal' forest.

The average length of ownership will be about 10 years. Gains on disposal of a property are the most normal way in which investors take their profits, but it doesn't matter too much at which points in the cycle you buy and sell since harvesting income and capital gains on disposal are given the same tax treatment.

Investors in the 1980s have lost money and timber prices had not risen during the nine years up to 2004. There are some signs now that both timber prices and forestry property values are recovering slightly.

How to invest

The key to successful investment in this market is the involvement of a competent manager who is fixed on the objective of making money. Investors should also look for an opportunity to buy in at a discount. This may not be too difficult because forestry valuers are highly conservative and will discount heavily anything that is not obviously of the best quality. Poorer quality timber may still be a good investment.

BULGARIA –
A PLACE IN SUN FROM £25,000

Bulgaria is rapidly becoming one of Europe's hottest locations for purchasing a second property, as it enjoys a stunning mix of historical heritage along with a wealth of new build development opportunities. Bulgarian Dreams, the UK's leading Bulgarian property agents, highlight that one of the reasons for the increase in Bulgaria's popularity is due to the perfect all year round climate, where it is possible to enjoy the gorgeous ski slopes in the winter and the miles of sumptuous sandy beaches in the summer. Two developments that are ideally situated for these activities are Cedar Lodge, just 5 minutes from the ski lift in Bansko, and Summer Dreams, located just 300 metres from the central Sunny Beach area.

Bulgarian Dreams have been involved with many Bansko developments and have been the sole selling agents for the already sold out Cedar Lodge I and Cedar Lodge II phases. Cedar Lodge III is now available and will be close to the main ski lift and as it is settled in a mountainous location, residents will enjoy spectacular views.

Bulgaria's coastline is nearly 350 kilometres long and stunning beaches can be found all along. The average top temperature in the summer is about 28°C, with sun from May to September. It is no wonder that Bulgaria has become such a popular summer destination. Summer Dreams is just 500 metres from central Sunny Beach and the 147 studio, one, two and three bedroom apartments and penthouses enjoy a secluded, wooded location.

Prices for the properties at Cedar Lodge III are starting at £25,000 for a studio apartment, whilst apartments at Summer Dreams start at £25,500. For further information on the properties at Cedar Lodge and Summer Dreams, as well as other developments currently available, please contact Bulgarian Dreams on, Tel: **020 7614 1240** or alternatively visit: **www.bulgariandreams.com**

Focus on buying where trees grow well, which means the western half of the United Kingdom where the rainfall is highest. There are more opportunities in Scotland than elsewhere, some in Wales and a few in the West Country. There are three ways that you can invest:

▍ *Individual investment* The minimum is about £50,000 but management costs can eat up much of the profit. Economies to scale only begin to apply nearer to £100,000 investment. If you can afford it, this is the preferred route. You may also benefit from non-forestry values such as recreation, camping, shooting and stalking, which you can develop for profit or simply to enjoy yourself.

▍ *Forestry investment partnerships* At the entry level with £40,000 or more to invest you could search out a manager who is prepared to set up a private partnership to acquire what he or she has assessed a potentially profitable forest property. Such an investment will probably be a mature plantation where harvesting income can be used to cover running costs. A typical forestry partnership will have four to eight investors and should include the manager to ensure that he or she has a personal interest in success.

▍ *Collective investment vehicles* Usually, they take the form of small trusts allowing modest levels of investment, as low as £1,000. Because of the small size management and regulatory costs are disproportionately high and the limited potential return makes such investment vehicles relatively unattractive.

The partnership route involves setting up a partnership to be dissolved at a specific future date, typically 10 to 15 years ahead. On dissolution the assets are sold and the proceeds distributed, free of tax, to the partners. Partnerships are usually fully funded when they are formed and there may be income distributions in the intervening years.

Fees on buying and selling

Most forestry investment is in freeholds. Like property generally, forestry is relatively illiquid. You are advised not to invest more than 10 to 15 per cent of your available capital in forestry.

When buying forestry it will probably take at least several months to locate and acquire commercial woodland to your specifications. If you employ an agent to act for you they will probably charge you a finder's fee of 1 to 2.5 per cent depending on the value of the property.

THE INCREDIBLE SCENTS AND THE RELAXED LIFESTYLE OF THE ISLAND
AWAITS YOU AT ORANGERY HOMES BY THE SEA...

ONLY 10 KM BY ASPHALT ROAD FROM THE CITY OF GIRNE, ORANGERY HOMES ARE
ARRANGED OVER A 40.140 M² AREA OVERLOOKING THE BEAUTIFUL NORTHERN
SHORES OF CYPRUS. THE UNIQUE PROJECT OFFERS 3 STYLES OF APARTMENTS
AND HOUSES THAT ARE DESIGNED TO GIVE YOU THE EXPERIENCE OF THE SIMPLE
YET WONDEROUS LIFESTYLE OF THE ISLAND. THE APPROACH OF THE FAMOUS
ARCHITECTS DILEKCI IS ABOUT COMPLETELY BLENDING IN AND FEELING AT ONE
WITH THE NATURAL SETTING AND SURROUNDS OF ORANGERY DEVELOPMENT.

ORANGERY
H O M E S   B Y   T H E   S E A

International Sales Office: Financial Dimensions Property

38 Park Street, Mayfair, London, W1K 2JF

T: 0044 20 7495 6000 · F: 0044 20 7495 8000 · E: info@fdlondon.com

www.orangeryhomes.com

Investing in Northern Cyprus

Referred to as a slumbering gold mine, Northern Cyprus is a jewel of the Mediterranean. Its beautiful shorelines are complimented with historic ruins and relics hidden in the mountains whilst lower hills hide woodland walks and rare species of birds and butterflies. Its warm climate is guaranteed and the welcome you receive is the reason you go back time and time again.

Property value is a British favourite, and the property market in Northern Cyprus is booming, and with outstanding value for money what better place to invest.

There are three main types of investors that look at Northern Cyprus.

1. Property purchaser – these are generally families investing in a holiday home or retired couples relocating to the Island.

2. But to Let Purchasers – properties purchased purely for investment. Rental income is generated from letting to holiday makers to the Island and occasionally to the locals. (expected rental yields are between 7-10% pa).

3. Land Purchases – Land purchasers fall in two categories a. small land purchases for a building a single dwelling for private use and b. large land purchases by developers and hoteliers.

Investments in Northern Cyprus can start from as little as °Í50,000.00, and payment plan schedules are generally available to make your purchase easier.

Please contact us at FD Property where you can find out more on how to invest in Northern Cyprus. We are ready to take you to a new world of investment opportunities.

FD Property

38 Park Street, Mayfair, London W1K 2JF
Tel: 0044 207 495 6000   Fax: 0044 207 495 8000
Email: property@fdlondon.com

When selling, expect to pay up to 2.5 per cent plus advertising costs to the agricultural department of a leading estate agent or a specialist forestry agency. The process will probably take some three to six months. Your manager may want to handle the sale in order to retain the management. Don't give him/her more than, say, four weeks before handing the sale over to the professionals.

Taxation benefits

The tax breaks on forestry investment are enticing.

▐ Timber income is free of income tax (and corporation tax if you are a limited company).
▐ Increases in the capital value of growing timber and gains on disposal are free of capital gains tax.
▐ Commercial woodlands are granted 100 per cent business property relief from inheritance tax after two years of ownership.

However, like houses, you are liable to pay stamp duty at the normal rates on forestry property acquisitions. Forestry business are subject to VAT.

Risks

The main risks are physical:

▐ Fire. The risk is slight and insurance is not expensive.
▐ Storm. Also insurable.
▐ Disease. Not insurable but good practice and alert management will contain such risks.

Of course, timber prices and forestry values are vulnerable to general economic factors. Political risk is limited to the possibility of a future Chancellor of the Exchequer deciding to abolish inheritance tax relief or tax forestry income and/or capital gains.

If investment in forestry is of interest to you, you might like to consult David Sillar of Highland Forestry Limited, from whose written work the content of this section is derived.

DISCOVER BODRUM

Enjoy the sheer beauty of Turkey and live your dreams. If you are looking for paradise, you have found it; Bodrum has it all.

It is obvious that nature has been generous to this magnificant coastal town in the Agean. Now, you can own beautiful apartments or villas from our wide range of homes with different specifications, sizes and locations in Bodrum.

We offer subsided inspection trips. Call now for further details:

FD Property
38 Park Street, Mayfair, London W1K 2JF
Tel: 0044 207 495 6000   Fax: 0044 207 495 8000
Email: property@fdlondon.com

Turkey – full of eastern promise

With the negotiations on EU membership scheduled and Turkey being a well recognised 'emerging market', now is a good time to invest.

For years Turkey has been a very popular tourist destination, now it seems it is becoming increasingly popular with property investors. Turkey offers more than enough opportunities for investors; good whether, yacht marinas, sandy beaches and golf courses but more importantly exceptional value for money.

Some areas have seen increases of up to 30% over the last year, and they are raising fast. The most popular areas at present are Alanya, Antalya, Bodrum, and Fethiye. As well as all these coastal destinations Istanbul boasting the Bosphorus together with its bustling bazaars and its historical & cultural events has fast become one of the most visited cities and the only one spanning both Europe and Asia. This has brought along with it an increase in property and development investment.

Mortgages are not readily available as yet in Turkey but are not far off. You will find that most developers have payment plans to assist in the purchase of your property these vary but typically you are required to make 20-30% deposit upon signing of contracts.

FD Property has a special relationship directly with the developers in Turkey and is here to guide you every step of the way, to elevate any apprehensions you may have.

To invest in turkey please call us now.

FD Property

38 Park Street, Mayfair, London W1K 2JF
Tel: 0044 207 495 6000   Fax: 0044 207 495 8000
Email: property@fdlondon.com

Business angel investment

Professor Colin Mason of the Hunter Centre for Entrepreneurship at the University of Strathclyde defines a business angel as 'someone who invests in unquoted, usually new or young, businesses in which there is no family connection'. However, as Professor Mason points out, business angel investments are high risk. Recent research indicates that 40 per cent of investments are loss-making and that, typically, the entire investment is lost. The same research suggests that a further 11 per cent do no better than break-even or fail to generate a return any better than that which you could have earned for your money in a bank account or other form of secure deposit.

Although 20 of the remaining 49 per cent of investments are said to generate internal rates of return (income plus capital gain) of more than 50 per cent, angel investment is clearly no place to put your money unless it represents no more than 10 to 15 per cent of your total investments.

Who should invest

Business angel investing is most suitable for business people with successful businesses from which they may already have exited, who are looking for another business in which to invest where they can play an active role, contributing their experience and skill as well as their cash investment.

Investments per company by business angels range from under £10,000 to over £100,000. Most angels have fewer than five investments in their portfolio, which experts would say is insufficient to spread their risk. Against that, business angels would argue that the time they have to take to evaluate investment opportunities and support those where they have invested makes it impossible to handle more. The ability to evaluate investment opportunities, structure investments and provide valuable hands-on support are real barriers to business angel investing as are time availability and the problem of finding suitable investment opportunities in the first place.

For wealthier individuals with the necessary skills, tax relief may provide an added incentive. If the business qualifies under the Enterprise Investment Scheme (EIS) and the investment can be structured within its rules, the investor can enjoy income tax relief at the 20 per cent rate on the amount invested up to £200,000. The investor can also enjoy gains on disposal free from capital gains tax, provided that the shareholding is less than 30 per cent and the shares have been held for a minimum of three years. Tax on capital gains from the sale of other assets can be deferred by reinvesting in an EIS company and any losses made on the disposal of EIS shares may also be offset against the capital gains made on others.

Arm's length investment

As with other classes of investment that we have considered in this chapter, there are ways in which you can put your money into angel investing as a more remote or 'dumb' investor:

■ *Venture capital trusts* A venture capital trust (VCT) is a quoted company that is similar to an investment trust but invested in a spread of unquoted companies, including companies listed on AIM, the junior London Stock Exchange market. The VCT managers make the decisions. Investments up to £200,000 in any tax year are eligible for 40 per cent income tax relief in the years 2004/05 and 2005/06. There is no CGT on disposals but losses are not allowed as capital losses. You can identify VCTs in the financial media, from financial advisers or on the web.

■ *Business angel syndicates* You can invest in a purely passive role in a business angel syndicate with a small core of active angel investors, usually supported by an investment manager. You will be one of the 'dumb investors' and will be relying on the judgement and experience of the hands-on members.

In all its forms, business angel investing is a risky business and probably not a suitable destination for your hard won windfall.

Checklist

1. The UK commercial property market is forecast to have produced returns of 9.8 per cent in 2004. You can enjoy the same returns as property investment funds and companies, provided that you can be sure of finding a tenant and that you only sign leases with fully commercial terms and conditions.

2. Residential property prices have slowed down or fallen since the bull market ran out in 2004, but house prices are forecast to rise again modestly later in 2005. There are still profitable niches in the buy-to-let market, such as direct student short lets and longer leases of student accommodation to universities.
3. Residential property buy-to-sell investments only escape CGT if the house is your PPR, but that won't work if you do it regularly when the Inland Revenue is likely to treat your profit as trading income.
4. As an alternative, you can buy shares in a company that is a house builder or supplies materials for building houses. You can also invest in a unit trust or OEIC that specializes in property or a new type of Property Investment Fund.
5. Residential property investment overseas is far more hazardous than in the United Kingdom. Be sure to use a properly qualified estate agent, lawyer and post-purchase service provider to manage the property.
6. Investors in forestry properties in the 1980s lost money but are showing signs of recovery. Timber prices returns can be improved up to 8 to 10 per cent a year tax-free with good management.
7. Entry level investment is at £40,000 minimum and a forestry investment partnership with four to eight investors in which the manager has a personal interest is probably the best route. Don't invest more than 10 to 15 per cent of your capital in forestry.
8. Timber income is free of income tax and gains on disposal are free of CGT. Commercial woodlands are 100 per cent free from inheritance tax after two years of ownership. The main risks are fire and storm (insurable) and disease.
9. Direct business angel investing is really for successful business people and experienced business professionals. Forty per cent of investments are loss-making where the entire investment is lost.
10. Arm's length investment in quoted Venture Capital Trusts carry tax advantages. You can also invest as a 'dumb investor' in a business angel syndicate where the decisions are taken by core active angel investors and a business manager. In every form, business angel investing is a risky business.

In 1980, the gold price hit an all time high of over $800 per troy ounce. The price had been rising steadily over previous months and investors who had bought gold when the price was low were reaping the profits. Now gold is trading at a mere $435 per ounce and investors are once more turning to gold as a viable investment. As with the Stock Market, the gold price can move up and down, but gold has always been considered both a safe haven in times of economic unrest, and also an instrument to vary stock portfolios.

At ATS Bullion, we have noticed a significant increase in the number of private investors buying gold over the past few months. People are concerned about low interest rates and the possibility of a fall in share prices. They want something tangible to tuck away for the future. Most gold coins and bars trade at a small premium over their metal value and unlike other investments, if the worst comes to the worst, they can be melted down for their metal content. Gold has always been the most desirable of all the precious metals. From the ancient Egyptians to modern day celebrities, it has always been seen as a symbol of wealth and success. Yet with prices of gold coins starting from as little as £30, you don't have to be a millionaire to enjoy ownership.

Finally, there is no VAT on investing in gold, making it more accessible for private buyers. The internet has made the gold price easy to follow and we find that people enjoy looking at our website to get a good idea of what they can buy before investing **(www.atsbullion.com)**. If you prefer to telephone us and have a chat about buying gold, our friendly and experienced dealers are always happy to advise you.

12 A little of what you fancy

The final class of investments are those that you want to make in non-business assets where you are the main decision-maker. Very often these will be related to your hobbies and pastimes where you are already quite knowledgeable. They will not produce an income but are still investments if you are using your specialist knowledge to invest in assets that will appreciate in value over time.

Here are just a few of the types of investment that you might consider, where it is possible to make worthwhile gains. If you are not already knowledgeable about them you can always set about getting to know them and studying sufficiently to become expert:

■ coloured diamonds;
■ art and antiques;
■ other collectibles;
■ racehorse ownership;
■ wine.

Coloured diamonds

Diamonds are considered by some to be the ultimate form of concentrated wealth. They are a private and transportable currency in themselves. In fact, we could have included them in the last chapter as a stable form of hands-on investment.

Coloured diamonds are a particularly sound investment. In the last 10 years, 24 out of the 25 highest prices paid at auction houses for gemstones and jewellery were for coloured diamonds. In the last quarter of 2004, the Gemological Institute of America (GIA) reported that the demand for them had risen 102 per cent since 1999. Pastor-Genève, the leading Geneva-based firm of coloured diamond dealers believes that the long-term potential for investment in coloured diamonds has never been stronger.

Valuation factors

The price at which you buy a diamond and its ability to increase in value is determined by its rarity. The main factors of rarity that influence prices are:

▌ *Colour* The colour saturation of the diamond is compared to the lightness or darkness of the colour to determine the grading. The stones at the top end of the grading spectrum are the rarest pieces with the strongest colour saturation and highest values.
▌ *Cut* The strongest influence on a diamond's brilliance is the cut. In a coloured diamond, the unique mixture of colour that the viewer experiences from the reflection of light entering the stone and reflecting back to the eye is termed 'face up colour'.
▌ *Carat weight* The standard unit of weight for diamonds and most other gems is the metric carat, equivalent to 0.2 grams. Coloured diamonds tend to appear in smaller sizes (seldom over one carat) than other diamonds and other gemstones.
▌ *Clarity* Coloured diamond connoisseurs tend to acquire a stone based on the colour saturation with clarity as a secondary consideration. Most diamonds contain 'inclusions' (internal imperfections) because of their chemical structure. Their concern is how the stone looks in natural sunlight compared with artificial light.

When purchasing a fancy coloured diamond, it is important that the stone has an origin-of-colour report from the GIA or another qualified gemological laboratory.

Rarity

Some colours are more or less rare than others. Of the estimated average 110 million carats of diamonds mined each year, only just over 2,000 carats will be cut and polished coloured diamonds (excluding browns and blacks).

In the coloured diamond marketplace, where buyers compete, coloured diamonds may be divided into three categories of rarity:

■ extremely rare: red, violet, green, blue;
■ rare: purple, pink, orange, olive, white;
■ moderately rare: grey, yellow, brown, black, colourless.

Stones classified as extremely rare are one-of-a-kind pieces and appear on the open market only a few times a year. However, stones classified as moderately rare, such as yellow diamonds and brown diamonds, have also seen dramatic sales increases because of their affordability, beauty and rarity compared with colourless diamonds.

Buying and selling coloured diamonds

Pastor-Genève reports that natural fancy yellow diamonds have doubled in value every nine years since the early 1970s against extremely rare blue diamonds that have doubled in value every five years.

If you are considering an investment in diamonds, Pastor-Genève recommends that you start your collection by investing £6,000 in one or two coloured diamonds in the moderately rare category. You have several options where to buy your coloured diamonds: retail jewellers, auction houses and speciality dealers. The third channel is preferable if you are purchasing in the rare and extremely rare categories, since speciality dealers have contacts directly at mines and are often in possession of stones unavailable at the retail level. They also maintain discretion and confidentiality for their clients.

If you choose to keep your diamonds in a bonded and insured storage facility abroad, the fees vary from a flat rate every year to a small percentage of the value of the stones. You should view coloured diamonds as a mid- to long-term investment for five years or more. When you want to sell, contact your dealer at least 90 days before you need the money. (The content of this section is drawn from a chapter contributed by Pastor-Genève to *The Handbook of Personal Wealth Management*, published by Kogan Page, 2005, ISBN 0 7494 4383 9.)

Art and antiques

The fine and decorative art market includes paintings, pictures, drawings, prints, sculpture, furniture, rugs and carpets, ceramics, glass, silver, clocks and watches, Oriental, Islamic, Russian and Indian works of art, and modern and contemporary art. There is a smaller market for collectibles, which we will look at in the next section.

The global art market in 2001 amounted to 1.2 million art transactions worldwide in which nearly £14 billion worth of fine and decorative art changed hands. The United States has 42 per cent of the global market, followed by the United Kingdom with 28 per cent. The UK art market is operated by 9,463 dealers and 754 auctioneers, which together employ more than 37,000 staff. London is the centre of the UK art business and in 2000 one London dealer alone handled 4 per cent of all UK dealer sales.

Don't be put off by the incredibly high prices that you read about for the paintings of the most acclaimed and fashionable painters. In 2002/03 alone 149 paintings were sold at auction for more than £1 million each, including 17 by living artists. Antique collecting and investment takes place at many price levels and can be a rewarding part of anyone's shopping experience as the BBC's *Antiques Roadshow* has demonstrated since the 1970s.

Factors in valuing art

The main factors in valuing art are:

■ artistic merit;
■ artist reputation;
■ provenance (ownership history and proof that it is genuine);
■ quality;
■ rarity;
■ condition;
■ fashion;
■ familiarity;
■ location;
■ size;
■ and, for very valuable works, museum buying power.

Subject matter can also make a difference to the price of a picture. Some of the features that can attract increased demand are beautiful young women and children in portraits, horses and figures in landscapes, dogs and game birds, flowers, sunny scenes or calm water, as well as bright, bold and pale colours.

Freshness on the market is also important. Items that may have appeared quite recently on the market are likely to be sold at a lower price than those that have been in a private collection for some years. The optimum collection period for investment purposes is said to be 20–30 years.

How to collect for investment

There are two main approaches that are recommended generally in collecting for investment purposes: specialization in a particular area or artist or specialization in an area that has remained unfashionable for years.

Many art experts would advise you to buy the best you can afford and to buy fewer pieces in the hope that your taste will prove to be the same as that of well-heeled buyers in the future. In the meantime, you may enjoy living with works of art that you bought because you like them. However, other long-term studies suggest that the more you pay, the lower the return. Therefore, if you intend to invest in an art portfolio, the best advice, as in conventional financial investments, may be to spread your money across more items. That way, you will spread the risk and enjoy a more diverse collection.

Unlike the investments that we studied in Part 4 and in the last chapter, the only return on investment in art or antiques comes as a capital gain when you sell. Therefore, the profit on sale after deducting acquisition and selling costs, valuation fees, insurance, conservation and storage costs must be greater to compare with other forms of investment. A recent study by Zurich Financial Services predicted that a painting bought at auction in 1997 for £1,000 net should fetch a sum of £2,159 in 2007, which would produce an 8 per cent compound annual return, including inflation at 3 per cent. Setting aside the enjoyment of collecting and the pleasure your investments will give you, you may conclude that there are other forms of investment that are more attractive.

Aids to investment

Information on the art market and art history is readily available from a number of UK publications. The leading weekly journal is *Antiques Trade Gazette* and monthlies include the *Art Newspaper, Art Review, Art Monthly, Apollo* and *Burlington.*

One of the best-known price guides since 1985, which many amateur collectors use as their bible, is *Miller's Antique Guide*, which covers 60 subjects and 10,000 items from 20 auctioneers. Prices include buyer's premium (the fee paid to the auction house on every transaction) and VAT.

If you want to study the market in more detail, art indexes provide a statistical analysis of the art market and its price movements over time. They record auction prices but may overlook dealers' prices, which are usually double. One of the oldest indexes is John Andrews' ACC index based on average prices for 35 types of 1,200 good quality pieces of British furniture from seven periods dating from 1650 to 1860.

Other UK indexes include Duncan Hislop's Art Sales Index, covering the fine art auction market and Robin Duthy's Art Market Research indexes (500 in all). There are also a number of informative English language websites located in France, the United States and Italy.

Buying and selling art

The main routes for art investors are via auctioneers, the internet, dealers and galleries, fairs, artists themselves and art funds. The UK auction market is dominated by Bonham's, Christie's and Sotheby's. There are also a number of provincial auctioneers and, of course, international internet auctioneers such as eBay.

Fees are an important consideration if you are buying or selling at auction. In the United Kingdom, Sotheby's charges sellers 15 per cent of the saleroom price plus 1.5 per cent for insurance. Bonham's charges 15 per cent for the first £1,000, 10 per cent between £1,000 and £70,000 and no commission above. Provincial auctioneers charge far less, but the standard of items on offer is generally lower.

Buyer's fees, which date from the 1970s are also heavy. Christie's and Sotheby's charge 19.5 per cent and 20 per cent respectively up to a £70,000 hammer price and from 10 to 12 per cent after that. Bonham's charges between 7.5 and 19.5 per cent up to £70,000 and then 10 per cent above.

Web sales and online auctions since August 1999 have become the most important development in the marketplace, especially for lower value items less than £5,000, which are now continuously accessible worldwide. In June 2004, eBay registered 114 million users, 51 per cent up on the previous year. The charges for using eBay are modest, £2 to list on the website and £20 once a £1,000 item has been sold.

Buying and selling through a dealer is a more straightforward trans-action and, if you are a buyer, you have a better opportunity to examine the item thoroughly. The downside is that prices at dealers' showrooms or fairs can be twice those paid at auctions. Nevertheless British dealers' collective turnover is still greater than the UK sales of the two main auction houses.

You will be wise to stick to those reputable dealers who are members of the British Antique Dealers' Association (BADA), the Association of Art and Antique Dealers (LAPADA) or the Society of London Art Dealers (SLAD). Members of all three are required to meet standards of knowledge, integrity and quality of stock and to offer a no-quibble guarantee to return your money in the event of making a mistake.

For the wealthy financial investor, there are a few professionally managed funds in which shares can be purchased. The Fine Art Fund in the United Kingdom demands a minimum investment of $250,000 and hopes to return 10–15 per cent compound annual growth after 10–13 years. Other recent Funds are ArtVest in Switzerland and Fernwood Art Investment in the United States. (The information for this section is drawn from art and antiques consultant and writer James Goodwin's chapter in *The Handbook of Personal Wealth Management*, referred to above.)

Collectibles

As those of you who are regular viewers of *Antiques Roadshow* will know, you can collect almost anything, and serious collections of the most unlikely objects may have a surprisingly high value. The definition of collectibles refers loosely to old cars, postage stamps, numismatic coins, outdated banknotes or stock certificates, manuscripts and letters from the famous, books, photographs, medals, playing cards, bric-a-brac, scientific instruments, firearms and other weapons, musical instruments, dolls and toys, luggage and many others.

You can buy many collectible items individually from a variety of sources including car boot sales, country house sales and various kinds of provincial antique shops at no great cost. Building the collection up steadily over time is a large part of the fun and does not require a major outlay at any stage.

Factors in valuation

The main factors in valuing collectibles are broadly the same as those listed above for art and antiques except, perhaps, artistic merit, although some collectible items are undoubtedly beautiful.

However, the rarity factor has special significance. For example, some makes and models of doll are particularly rare because very few were made and you would need to know your subject thoroughly when buying to tell which they were. Very possibly, the seller would not know unless they specialized in dolls, and this presents you with a challenge and an opportunity to make a decent profit. Rare dolls sell commonly for several thousands of pounds.

Similarly, a toy made as recently as the 1970s may have a real value because the design was only current for a short period and was replaced by a similar design with slightly different features. Enthusiastic youngsters are particularly well-informed collectors and are often aware of these differences.

As well as condition, another important element in establishing highest value is the original packaging in which the product was supplied. Collectors who have retained the manufacturer's packaging can add greatly to the value of their hoard.

Serious investors in collectibles tend to focus on higher value items. Vintage and veteran motor cars were a fashionable investment in the 1970s and 1980s, partly because their owners could enjoy driving as well as owning them. However, that market crashed in the 1990s and has not really recovered, although some very rare post-war models and the rarer pre-World War II classics still command very high prices.

One interesting and somewhat neglected field for investment is string instruments and bows. Wind and brass instruments depreciate, but string instruments appreciate in value. For a few thousand pounds you can buy an old violin that will almost certainly increase its value. Above £30,000 you can buy an instrument or bow by a well-known maker with full provenance, having a maker's label inside the violin or engraved into the heel of the bow. Such an investment is almost guaranteed to appreciate. They are bought and sold at all of the big London auction houses. There are also specialist London dealers like Beare's, Guiver's and Ealing Strings and the monthly magazine, *The Strad*, carries their advertisements.

For many people, the attraction of investing in string instruments is not just that they appreciate in value, but also that the owners can lend their instruments to young professional players or students (suitably insured, of course) who cannot afford a good instrument themselves. (You may even have a talented violinist in your family.) This is quite a common practice. A few years ago, there was a well-publicized example of a multi-millionaire who lent 12 Stradivarius violins to members of the New Jersey Symphony Orchestra – ensuring that at least its violin section would produce a high quality sound!

When choosing your field of collectibles, the best advice is to buy into something because you like it, or that appears undervalued on the price information that you have. Then sit back and enjoy collecting until prices rise and you decide reluctantly that the time has come to sell.

Racehorse ownership

The breeding and sale of prospective racehorses is a big business in the United Kingdom worth billions of pounds. There are some 14,000 race-horses in training, which are the product of a global horse breeding industry. Racehorse ownership is hardly a general route to profitable investment but there are ways of making big money from investing in thoroughbreds.

One surprising fact about the bloodstock or horse breeding industry is that nearly every racehorse can be traced back through the breeding records to the founding fathers of modern horse racing, three Arab stallions that were imported into Britain between 1688 and 1730. There are five 'classic' races in Britain, all on the flat, starting with the Derby, first run in 1780, and then the 1,000 Guineas, 2,000 Guineas, the Oaks and the St Leger. Racing over obstacles (chases and hurdles) were introduced in the mid-19th century. The Grand National is the best-known chase.

There are 59 racecourses in Britain and total prize money reached a record total of £95 million in 2003. In 2004, 1,341 race meetings were scheduled, providing nearly 8,500 races. Some 60,000 people are employed in racing and breeding and a further 40,000 in the betting industry where about two-thirds of the profits come from horse racing.

Investment opportunities

At present there are more than 9,500 active racehorse owners in the United Kingdom and about 50,000 people involved through various types of co-ownership. You can derive great pleasure from owning part or all of a racehorse, but should view it as a hobby rather than an investment. Occasionally, large profits can be made, but these are few and far between.

Buying a horse will often cost more than £10,000 and the annual cost of having a horse in training is around £16,000. A few recover their costs in prize money, but the more usual way to make money from a horse in training is to sell it on at a profit to race for another owner or to sell it for breeding as a stallion or broodmare prospect.

You are unlikely to want or to be able to buy a racehorse by yourself, but it is possible to invest in a syndicate. If four of you buy a horse together, it can be said that you each own 'a leg'. Meticulous details of every thoroughbred horse are kept in the General Stud Book, held and maintained by Weatherbys. Training fees and management costs charged by the syndicate organizers are the main part of the ongoing cost burden and there is no certainty that they will be matched by any financial return.

The other way to invest in horses (we refer briefly to betting on the nags in Chapter 14) is to join in a syndicate that buys a horse, either a foal, yearling or mare and resells it at a later date. This activity is known as 'pinhooking' and you can focus on any or all of the stages in the cycle from foals to yearlings, yearling to two-year-olds in training, fillies (female horses up to the age of four) to broodmares or buying a mare and selling the foals from her. Again, this is not a licence to print money but many more people make money by trading in bloodstock than through racehorse ownership.

If you are interested in joining a pinhooking syndicate, the best way to select an agent or adviser is through personal recommendation or to ask the British Horseracing Board for guidance.

Investing in wine

This is one investment field where you really do need to take expert advice or become an expert yourself – not too unpleasant a labour! If you are buying to invest, rather than for drinking, the following are a basic set of rules:

- Only buy from the best vintages (the year in which the grapes were harvested and the wine made).
- Only buy wines from vineyards that have a proven track record of increased prices for their wines in good vintages.
- Check that the wine has been reviewed and scored well on the points scale of Robert Parker, the American wine writer in his journal *The Wine Advocate*.
- Purchase only from reputable wine merchants and brokers.

Across the board, the red wines from the Bordeaux region of France, sometimes called 'claret' in the United Kingdom, have accounted for more good wine investments than any other. If you had bought a 12-bottle case of Château Pétrus 1982 in 1983 you would be able to sell it today for about £17,000 and there would be no capital gains tax, because the Inland Revenue classifies wine as an article with a finite life of less than 50 years. But that, of course, is an extreme example.

Best practice for wine investors

There are a number of sound practices that you are recommended to observe when you invest in wine, as follows:

■ *Time frame* A minimum of five years is a reasonable time to keep the wines that you buy. You may want to drink some and sell some with the prospect of getting the drinking portion 'free' if you have bought well. Ten years is better, because any downturns in world markets are more likely to be smoothed out.

■ *Wine selection* For investment, it is better to purchase one case of wine costing £1,000 rather than five at £200 a case. Each case will cost about £9 per year in cellar charges.

■ *Storage* Purchase your wine in original wooden cases (owc), which are the same cases in which it left the winery. Loose bottles, even when assembled in dozens and packed into other cases are worth at least 10 per cent less than those in their original cases. The selection of a quality cellarer is also critical.

■ *Duty and VAT* When you purchase wine, be sure that it is 'in bond' – that is, lying in a cellar under the supervision of HM Revenue & Customs. That way you defer paying duty at about £15 a case and VAT at 17.5 per cent until you decide to sell or drink the wine.

■ *Provenance* It is best to buy a case of wine that came into the United Kingdom directly from the château and lay undisturbed in one cellar.

■ *Older vintages of wine* Make sure that wines older than 10 years are checked carefully for condition including the levels in individual bottles, the labels, the capsule and the wine box itself. Leaking and protruding corks can indicate heat damage.

Robert M. Parker, Jnr, referred to above, argues persuasively why you should consider wine as an investment:

No matter how high prices appear today for wines from the most hallowed vineyards, they represent only a fraction of what these wines will fetch in a decade... If my instincts are correct, 10 years from now, a great vintage of the first growth Bordeaux 2003 will cost over $10,000 a case... at the minimum.

(The advice on buying wine follows the recommendations of Soorat Singh of Dunbar Fine Wines.)

A charitable thought

Finally, while reviewing what you fancy for non-business investment, you might want to think about sharing some of your good fortune with a registered charity, perhaps one that you already support from time to time.

The most effective way to contribute to any charity, provided that it is registered, is to enter into a Deed of Covenant in favour of the chosen charity, for a minimum period of four years under which you contract to pay a regular amount each year from your taxed income by monthly, quarterly or annual instalments. With this arrangement you also complete Inland Revenue Form R185(Covenant), a certificate of tax deducted, which enables the charity to claim back the tax you paid at the basic rate.

For example, the basic rate of tax for the year 2004/05 was 22 per cent. Therefore, the tax deducted on a payment to charity of £100 in that tax year was £28.20. When claimed back, your actual contribution to the charity was increased to £128.20. Not exactly a return on your investment, but money back from the taxman is surely the next best thing!

Checklist

1. Coloured diamonds are almost a currency in themselves. The main factors of rarity that influence price are colour, cut, carat weight and clarity. Make sure that any fancy coloured diamond that you buy has an origin-of-colour report from a qualified laboratory.

2. Start your coloured diamond collection by investing in one or two in the moderately rare category. Fancy yellow diamonds have doubled in value every nine years since the 1970s.

3. Don't be put off by the high prices of world class art. Specialize in a particular area or artist but spread your money across more items rather than less. Paintings bought at auction for £1,000 in 1997 are tipped to fetch £2,159 in 2007, but don't forget the high fees and costs of buying and selling.

4. If you are buying through dealers, stick to members of the reputable associations BADA, LAPADA or SLAD.

5. When choosing your field of collectibles, buy into something because you like it or that appears to be undervalued. Then sit back and enjoy your collecting.

6. Few racehorse owners recover their costs in prize money but hope to make money from a horse in training by selling it on. You will probably prefer to invest in a syndicate rather than own a horse yourself. There is no assurance that any financial return will match the training fees and management costs.

7. You can join a syndicate that engages in 'pinhooking' – buying a foal, yearling or mare and selling it at a future date. More people make money by trading in bloodstock than by owning racehorses.

8. When buying wine take expert advice and follow the basic rules. Red wines from the Bordeaux region of France are generally the best investment bet.

9. Five years is the minimum period to keep a wine, if you intend to drink part of the profit, but 10 years is better. Be sure to purchase your wine in the original wooden cases and to leave it in bond until you decide to drink or sell.

10. Consider sharing your good fortune by a donation to charity through a four-year covenant, which will enable the charity to claim back the income tax you paid on the amount of your donation.

Part Six
Financial health warnings

13 Scams and swindles

Of the two chapters in this final part of the book, this one is appropriately numbered 13. In it you will find a summary of the perils you face from scams and swindles designed by fraudsters and others to rob you of your money. There's an old saying 'A fool and his money are soon parted', usually directed at people who have come into unaccustomed wealth. In this electronic age you don't have to be a fool to become a victim to fraud and deception, but you do have to be careful. The message of this chapter is: if you've had a windfall, be sure that you keep it while you are deciding whether to save or spend.

Saving and investment alerts

Some financial products, particularly those that are advertised heavily to the public, should be approached with extreme caution until you are sure that you are aware of and understand exactly what is being offered. All too often the information provided by the advertiser is incomplete, misleading or both.

Exotic ISAs

Towards the end of the tax year, the newspapers are full of advertisement for ISA investments, some of them definitely 'exotic'. Just because it is the end of the tax year, don't be tempted to rush in and sign on the dotted line. Look at the 'wrapper' too. Just because a product is packaged as an ISA, that doesn't mean that it is a simple investment. ISAs can include high risk products that may have potential for a high return but usually mean a higher risk to your money.

High income ISAs

ISAs advertising 'guaranteed' high income also carry risks. They may not be able to maintain the level of income advertised without eating into the money you originally invested (your capital). Alternatively, they may offer a higher potential rate of return because the underlying investments are riskier, such as high income bonds.

ISA guides

You will sometimes see advertisements for ISA guides in the press. They are usually sponsored by firms and often don't explain clearly the recommendations that they make. ISAs recommended in these guides are not necessarily suitable for you.

Hedge funds and derivatives

Small savers are currently offered ISAs that invest in hedge funds or use derivatives linked to the performance of a complex hedge fund index. They are difficult to understand and charges may not be clear. You should avoid them.

Scams and frauds by telephone or mail

Share scams

Take care if a stranger rings you up and tries to sell you shares in companies of which you've never heard. They may be using hard-sell tactics to persuade you to buy shares as part of a scam. If you do buy in the end, you may be left with worthless shares and no rights to claim for compensation.

You may also hear first from such scam artists by post or e-mail. Beware of accepting any free research into companies where you have shares already, or free gifts or a discount on their dealing charges. If you sign on any dotted line, you may be letting yourself in for something quite different, which is in the small print only. And, if you are comforted by the UK freepost address on the envelope, remember that may be just a collection address for onward transmission to an overseas address.

Financial scams operating in the United Kingdom are usually closed down quickly by the FSA, whose consumer protection rules are strong. But protection abroad is far from identical. Remember that financial scamsters operating from overseas are able to correspond with UK investors or investors anywhere around the world. If a caller from abroad invites you to buy shares, the only appropriate reaction is to slam down the phone.

Advance fee scams

Have you received one of those official-looking letters through your letterbox offering you a fortune if you will help the sender to transfer millions of pounds out of their country? Some great misfortune in their country or the fact that they have become a political refugee may be given as the reason. You will be asked to send details of your bank account and an administration fee to initiate the transaction in return for a large commission on the funds to be transferred through your account. You might find the same sort of message when you open the mailbox for your e-mail from what appears to be a national bank or some other reputable institution.

This kind of swindle, which surfaced first in the 1980s, used to be called 'the Nigerian scam' because many of the requests purported to come from Nigeria at a time when that country had unstable government. Wherever the communication comes from, be very clear. The money does not exist.

Affinity fraud

Investment scams that target members of a group, such as the elderly, members of a profession, or religious or ethnic communities, even the congregation of a particular church or an old people's club classify as affinity fraud. Often the swindler will claim to be a member of the group. Sometimes, they will actually join the group in order to have access to its members. The internet has made life easier for this type of fraudster. Circulating members of a specific group by e-mail where addresses are known or contacting websites, bulletin boards and chat rooms devoted to them is quick and cheap.

Pyramid schemes

This form of fraudulent scheme is an old favourite to which many of us may have been exposed. Recruitment usually takes place in pubs or private homes where new recruits, invited by family and friends, are told that they can convert a sum of money, say, £1,000 into £10,000 in a few days. All you have to do is to hand over your money and secure new recruits to the scheme enabling the original recruits to move up a level in the pyramid. When you reach the top of the pyramid and receive your £10,000 you leave the scheme and make way for a new intake of 'winners'.

The schemes are called pyramid schemes because the money works its way up to a few people at the top and it's only those people who receive the financial benefit. The scheme only goes on working so long as there is an inexhaustible supply of people who are prepared to join at the base of the pyramid in order to push those who joined earlier towards the top. Sooner or later, the supply of recruits (and money) dries up and those who have money in the scheme at that time won't get it back.

Chain letters

The chain letter is another old chestnut that you may even have come across at school. You receive a letter or e-mail out of the blue asking you to send, say, £10 to the person at the top of the list and inviting you to put your name on the list , photocopy the letter and send it out to, say 200 people. According to the letter, you will receive a guaranteed return of £400,000 for your initial £10 outlay.

The mechanics are much the same as a pyramid scheme. The only way that you will ever recover any money is to recruit more members who will all pay the same, and recruit even more members and so on.

Identity fraud

In 2004, there were 13,000 recorded cases of identity fraud in the United Kingdom, nearly eight times as many as in 1999. Identity fraud is where someone impersonates you without your knowledge or consent, or uses your personal information, in order to obtain money, goods or services. Criminals are estimated to gain £1.4 billion a year from identity fraud. If your identity has been stolen, you may find debt collectors demanding payment of debts that aren't yours, bills arriving for accounts you don't have and even your applications for credit refused.

How your identity can be stolen and exploited

The most obvious way to have your identity stolen is through the theft of your wallet or handbag. Even your cheque book, mobile phone a few items of mail may be enough to get the fraudsters started, particularly if they can find your date of birth and then use public records to discover your birthplace and your mother's maiden name. (Far too many people give their mother's maiden name as a password for entry to their credit card telephone centres.)

When you cancel your credit cards, you may actually be helping the thieves to carry out their fraud. Using your personal details they may intercept your new card, write cheques from your chequebook and pay them into your new cards before using them to extract cash.

'Bin raiding' as a method of identity fraud has received much recent publicity. A survey carried out by Experian, the consumer credit agency, found that one in 10 people throw out in their rubbish a complete combination of credit or debit card number, expiry date, issue number and signature. Since some companies don't ask for the three-digit code on the back of the card, that information may be enough for the fraudster to start using your identity online to purchase goods and services. The criminal could also call a credit provider, substitute a new address and then order new cards.

Using a small handheld electronic reader, a fraudster could also read the magnetic strip on your card when you are buying something in a shop and then produce a brand new card for their own use. The great benefit to the criminal of this method is that you remain unaware of what's happening.

Even 'previous address fraud' is not uncommon. When you sell your house, dishonest new owners might use your name to order goods on credit and then tell the debt collectors that you had moved.

Virtual fraud

The internet, and e-mails in particular, have opened up the opportunity for entirely new criminal activity. Hackers can implant viruses in spam e-mails that access sensitive information on your PC.

Cold calling is another favourite technique. Typically, you receive a phone call one evening or early one morning from your 'bank' when you are likely to be busy. They tell you that they suspect your card has been used fraudulently and are checking up to see whether you have made a certain transaction. Then they take you through your security details, including your PIN number and your mother's maiden name (see above). Never hand over your security details unless you have contacted your bank yourself. A genuine call or e-mail from your bank should never ask you for them.

Precautions

Experts in the field of fraud prevention suggest some simple steps that you can take to reduce the risk of identity theft:

▌ Don't carry documents around unless you need to. For example, leave your driving licence at home unless you're hiring a car.

▌ Don't ever carry your address in your wallet.

▌ Keep your bank details and identity documents locked up. If not, don't keep them altogether in one place, making it easy for a burglar.

▌ Don't use the same password on more than one bank account and don't use the same password on your credit cards (particularly obvious ones like your mother's maiden name or the name of a child).

▌ Shred all old documents with identity details including bank and credit card statements, even electricity bills or anything with an account or reference number, which can be used to give instructions or make commitments in your name.

A recent *Which?* magazine survey found that only 31 per cent of respondents both shredded documents and used different passwords; 33 per cent took neither precaution.

Internet fraud

Gone phishing

'Phishing' refers to a criminal scam to trick internet users into disclosing personal financial account information, username, password or other information leading to identity theft and fraud. A phishing scam uses e-mail and a website designed to represent well-known legitimate businesses, such as your bank, other financial institutions and government agencies. It is the internet equivalent of cold calling and is called 'phishing' because the fraudsters are trying to 'phish' victims from a sea of internet users.

According to one survey, phishing attacks targeted 57 million internet users worldwide in 2004. On average, three to five per cent of all individuals who received a phishing e-mail responded and became victims of the fraud.

It's very difficult to tell whether or not you have received fake e-mails because they are carefully designed to look like those of the organization from which they are pretending to have been sent. The following are some of the preventative actions you can take:

▌ Be suspicious of any e-mails with urgent requests for personal financial details.
▌ Call the organization concerned to check that they sent the e-mail.
▌ Check your online accounts regularly to make sure that there are no unexplained transactions.
▌ Check your bank and credit card statements regularly.
▌ Never use links within an e-mail to reach a company's website. It's safer to type in the company's website address.
▌ Always report the phishing e-mail to the company concerned when detected.
▌ Keep your anti-virus software up to date. That way you will download the latest spam filters, which can stop the kind of spam through which many phishing scams are transmitted.

Internet auction sites

Internet auctions have become increasingly popular and a way of life for some bargain seekers. Reputable auction sites like eBay have developed an enormous worldwide trade and offer an intriguing new marketplace as well as providing good fun for the family.

However, internet auction sites are not always what they seem and there are all too many cases of customers receiving nothing, having paid up front. As phishing activity grows, you also have to ask yourself whether you are comfortable providing your credit card or debit card details on the internet.

Bulletin boards and chat rooms

Thousands of messages are posted on internet bulletin boards daily in chat rooms offering tips on shares. Most are innocent, but some turn out to be phoney or even scams.

In principle, financial chat rooms and bulletin boards are internet sites where professional and personal investors alike can exchange news and views on the stock market. As the FSA points out, it's rather like exchanging gossip on which shares to buy in your local pub. But do you always believe everything you hear in the pub?

The difference from your local pub is the sheer number of people worldwide who can access the information and the speed at which the notices can be posted. You should also remember that you're 'chatting' to complete strangers who could be anyone.

These chat rooms and bulletin boards can be used by the unscrupulous to 'talk up' companies in which they hold shares in order to encourage you to buy shares too and thereby boost the price. They then sell their shares to make a quick profit and, in the absence of more buying, the share price goes down and so does the value of your shareholding. This kind of scam has earned the name of 'pumping and dumping' and there are cases already in the United States. If you are sucked into a pumping and dumping scam, you will find it an excellent way to lose money fast.

14 Gambling

This book would hardly be complete without a few words about 'gambling'. You have travelled through a series of chapters providing information and, hopefully, some worthwhile advice on how to keep and where to put your money. The ground we have covered includes:

■   successful spending;
■   canny credit;
■   low cost loans;
■   secure saving;
■   intelligent investment in securities;
■   active investment involvement.

And, in the last chapter, a series of cautions how not to have your money taken from you. Gambling is the final way in which you can decide to use and lose your money.

If you lose money on gambling, remember that it is a self-inflicted loss however much you kid yourself that you took a series of logical decisions to invest in calculated risk. If you want to have a 'flutter', that's your choice, but there's one golden rule. *Decide before you start how much you are prepared to lose, and never exceed your limit.*

Informed betting

Basically, there are two forms of gambling: informed betting and playing the odds. You can come equally unstuck on either but informed betting is the more seductive because it introduces an element of real or imagined reasoning into your betting process.

The old-fashioned football pools was the commonest form of informed betting although some punters chose to make their selections with a pin, draw tickets out of a hat or go through some other routine of random selection. Others studied carefully the past performance and results of the teams playing against the same or other opponents, this season or last season, home or away or since the acquisition of a new star player compared to the period before. They then based their selections on an analysis of the evidence, giving weight to those factors that they considered the most important.

Looked at this way, and if you are prepared to spend considerable time studying 'the form' then you are placing a series of informed bets when you pick winning teams. You can also read what football commentators in the newspapers or on TV say, and include that in your judgement.

If only betting were so easy! Sadly, however logical your judgement, there are factors at play that reduce your informed bet to a gamble. The weather, the state of the pitch, last minute or on the field injuries, players – or even the whole team – off form, any of these unforeseeable circumstances can make your homework count for nothing.

The same is of course true, but even more so, in the case of horse racing where published form books and mathematical calculations are available to the serious punter. Bookmakers set the odds that they are prepared to accept on each horse in each race, which move up and down according to the weight of the actual betting and there are often a considerable number of runners. So, one of the judgements that you have to make is whether the bookies odds are over-estimating or under-estimating the chances of each horse and its rider.

Racing 'over the sticks', with the possibility of mishaps and collisions while jumping fences, adds additional risks to picking a winner. However, in gambling on horses there are some opportunities to change the odds for your own bet. If there are sufficient runners you can make a place or 'each way' bet, which should get your money back if the horse you have chosen comes in the first three past the post. You can also hedge your bets with spread betting or deliberately increase the odds with accumulator bets in order to earn a higher reward on a lower stake if all the horses that you have picked for a series of races romp home as winners.

In spite of all the unpredictable elements in weather, ground conditions and equine behaviour, there are some almost professional punters who study the form hard, have good judgement and earn themselves a regular return on backing horses. They will lose some bets but win more and that gives them a continuing income. Unless you are one of these, you would be unwise to view horse race betting as any kind of income producer.

Card games are in another category. Playing bridge or poker with consistent success involves both a first-class memory of which cards have been played and an understanding of the odds in each set of circumstances. There is still a strong element of guesswork in deciding which of the unplayed cards are held by the players round the table, but for a skilled professional card player the odds can be reduced to a minimum. The one part that is completely outside your control is the initial distribution of cards at the beginning of either game – unless you are an accomplished cardsharp and happen to be dealing! Again, the leading international bridge and poker players often make a good living from their game.

Playing the odds

Where judgement plays no part in improving the likely result of a gamble because the selection process is entirely random, that is, there are no external circumstances or human intervention that can tilt the odds one way or the other, you are making a pure gamble. The outcome may be said to depend entirely on the laws of probability, and you need to understand how these work before you decide whether or not to place a bet.

The meaning of probability

Probability identifies for us the likelihood of something happening. Events or outcomes are likely to happen with a particular probability that can be defined mathematically.

There are some things that you may say are almost certain to happen, and to these you can give a probability of 100 per cent. Equally, the probability given to an event that will never happen is zero.

Examples of 100 per cent probability, which can also be classed as a probability of 1, are:

I   The sun will rise tomorrow morning.
I   If you pick a card from a pack (excluding jokers) it will be either a 'red card' or a 'black card'.
I   Fresh flowers in a vase will die.

Examples of zero probability (a probability of 0) are:

- running 50 miles in an hour;
- throwing a zero with a dice;
- the cow jumping over the moon.

All probabilities can be given a score according to a scale of 0 to 1 or 0 per cent to 100 per cent. Anyone who tells you that an event is so certain that it is '110 per cent probable' is exaggerating.

We can say that some events have an even or 50–50 chance of happening. The probability is ½, which can be written as 0.5 or 50 per cent. Examples are:

- the probability of getting a head when a British coin is tossed;
- the probability of drawing a red card from a pack;
- the chance of a slice of buttered toast landing butter side up. (I'm not too confident about the last example. Mine always seem to land butter side down!)

In practice, a 50 per cent probability does not mean that when you get one result the first time, you will get the alternative result next time. When you toss a coin 100 times, although the probability is that you will get 50 heads, it doesn't mean that you will get exactly 50 heads and 50 tails. With a lesser number of throws you are even less likely to get a 50/50 result. Over a much larger number of throws, say 1000, you would expect to get close to 500 heads and 500 tails. If you only get 300 or 30 per cent, it is likely that the coin is biased (weighted unevenly).

Probabilities in daily life

The next point to understand is that:

the probability that an event does *not* occur = 1 – the probability that it does occur.

As an example, a pessimist might say that 'it is 60 per cent likely to rain tomorrow', whereas an optimist could say 'there's a 40 per cent (100 per cent – 60 per cent) chance that it will stay dry'.

There are many probabilities that can only be calculated by carrying out a survey or looking at past performance. In terms of past events,

the probability = $\dfrac{\text{the number of events or incidents of relevance}}{\text{the number of possible incidents}}$

In an example based on road traffic deaths in 2000, out of the UK population of 60 million, 3,000 people were killed. It follows that the probability of being killed in a road accident in 2000 was approximately:

$$\frac{3,000}{60,000,000}$$

$$\frac{1}{20,000} \text{ (or 1 in 20,000)}$$

Winning the National Lottery

The probability of winning the jackpot on the National Lottery is quite a complicated calculation. As you know, it is the probability of choosing six numbers out of a possible 49. You pick six numbers and these are your chances as each ball is chosen:

The probability of the 1st ball being correct = $\frac{6}{49}$ (6 possible choices) (49 possible balls)

The probability of the 2nd ball being correct = $\frac{5}{48}$ (5 possible choices) (48 possible balls)

The probability of the 3rd ball being correct = $\frac{4}{47}$

The probability of the 4th ball being correct = $\frac{3}{46}$

The probability of the 5th ball being correct = $\frac{2}{45}$

The probability of the 6th ball being correct = $\frac{1}{44}$

Since all six numbers must be correct to win, all six probabilities must be multiplied so that:

The probability of winning = $\dfrac{6 \times 5 \times 4 \times 3 \times 2 \times 1}{49 \times 48 \times 47 \times 46 \times 45 \times 44}$

$$= \frac{1}{13,983,816}$$

Therefore, the probability of winning the jackpot is about 1 in 14 million.

Plainly, playing the National Lottery is not an investment. You could regard it as your contribution to charity since much of the money raised each week is allocated to charity and community projects. However, like me, you may not feel entirely in sympathy with many of the projects that are supported.

Full circle

Discussion of the National Lottery brings us back to where we started at the beginning of this book. When identifying the different ways in which you might have acquired the additional cash, which prompted you to ask the question 'Where to put my money?' we included the National Lottery. If you were a lottery jackpot winner, you might as well try again. The odds of winning are 1 in 14 million each time you play. The laws of probability take no account of previous wins. On the other hand, if you have never won, you are no more likely to next time you play. The odds are not improved by every failure to win. Perhaps the best argument for playing each week is that 'somebody always wins, even if it is from a rollover'.

If winning on the National Lottery is a matter of extreme luck, using any spare cash that you have accumulated wisely is certainly not. I hope that in this book we have demonstrated how to extract satisfaction from spending or saving your spare cash. The range of alternative investments discussed may also give you ideas how to invest your windfall with the degree of risk that is acceptable to you.

Appendix:
Useful websites and
e-mail contacts

Active Investments

Art, Antiques and Collectibles
jamesgoodwin@hotmail.com

Coloured Diamonds
mike@pastor-geneve.com

Racehorse Ownership
cwilson@bhb.co.uk

Wine
info@dunbarfinewine.co.uk

Personal Banking

www.alliance-leicester.co.uk

www.barclaysbank.co.uk

www.halifax.co.uk

www.hsbc.co.uk/hsbc/personal

www.lloydstsb.com

www.rbs.co.uk

www.scottishwidows.co.uk

Credit Reference Agencies

www.callcredit.plc.uk

www.equifax.co.uk

www.experian.co.uk

Financial Investments

Lloyds TSB Private Banking
john.dawe@lloydstsb.co.uk

Self-Investment Ltd
andrew@self-investment.com

UBS Laing & Cruickshank Ltd
Lisa.barp@lacim.co.uk

Weston Financial Management
Andy.Kinnard@bbnfp.co.uk

Financial Services Authority

www.fsa.gov.uk/consumer

www.childtrustfund.gov.uk

Hands-on Investments

Cordea Savills
info@cordeasavills.com

Stop Think Investment Group
mark@oceanviewpropertiesgroup.com

Highland Forestry Limited
highfieldforestry@btinternet.com

Hunter School of Entrepreneurship, University of Strathclyde
colin.mason@strath.ac.uk

National Savings & Investments

www.nationalsavings.co.uk

www.nsandi.co.uk

Pensions

www.pensioncalculator.co.uk

www.stakeholderhelpline.org.uk

www.fsa.uk/consumer/decision_trees/mn_stakeholder.html

The Stationery Office Books

www.stationeryoffice.co.uk

Which? magazine on credit cards

www.which.co.uk/creditcards

Advertisers' web addresses

Index

Index of advertisers

Further reading from Kogan Page

An A-Z of Finance: A Jargon Free Guide to Investment and the City, Michael Becket, 1998

The Complete Guide to Buying and Selling Property: How to get the best deal on your home, 2nd edition, Sarah O'Grady, 2004

The Complete Guide to Buying and Renting Your First Home, 3rd edition, Niki Chesworth, 2004

The Complete Guide to Buying Property Abroad, 4th edition, Liz Hodgkinson, 2005

The Complete Guide to Buying Property in France, 3rd edition, Charles Davey, 2005

The Complete Guide to Buying Property in Italy, Barbara McMahon., 2004

The Complete Guide to Buying Property in Portugal: Buying, Renting, Letting, Selling, Colin Barrow, 2005

The Complete Guide to Buying Property in Spain, Charles Davey, 2005

The Complete Guide to Family Finance: Essential Advice on Everything from Student Loans to Inheritance Tax, Roderick Millar, 2004

The Complete Guide to Letting Property, 5th edition, Liz Hodgkinson, 2005

The Complete Guide to Renovating and Improving Your Property, Liz Hodgkinson, 2004

Fear and Loathing in My Bank Account: Money Matters for the Financially Challenged, Sean Coughlan, 2002

The Good Non Retirement Guide 2005: Leisure, Health, Pensions, Tax, Holidays, Jobs, Investment, Voluntary Work and Much More, 19th edition, Rosemary Brown, 2005

The Independent Schools Guide 2005–2006, 12th edition, Gabbitas Educational Consultants, 2005

The Joy of Money, Michelle Doughty, 2006

How the Stock Market Works: A Beginner's Guide to Investment, 2nd edition, Michael Becket, 2004

How to Understand the Financial Pages, Alexander Davidson, 2005

How to Win as a Stock Market Speculator Trading, Technical Analysis, Financial Spread Betting, 2nd edition, Alexander Davidson, 2006

How to Win in a Volatile Stock Market: The Definitive Guide to Investment Bargain Hunting, Alexander Davidson, 2002

How to Write Your Will, 15th edition, Marlene Garsia, 2006

Living and Working in France: Chez Vous en France, 3rd edition, Geneviève Brame, 2004

Schools for Special Needs 2005–2006: A Complete Guide, 11th edition, Gabbitas Educational consultants, 2005

The Student Finance Guide: Fees, Grants and What it Costs, Sean Coughlan, 2005

The 10-Week Flexible Investment Plan: A Beginner's Guide to Stockmarket Success, Alexander Davidson, 2001